Table of Contents

About the Stories

Through biographies and realistic fiction, students will learn about people, events, and ideas that represent the grand diversity of the people of North America.

While providing reading practice, the 19 stories in *Read and Understand, Celebrating Diversity, Grades 2–3* present ideas and information that address diversity objectives in current standards outlined by the National Council for the Social Studies.

The stories in this book progress from second- to fourth-grade reading levels. When dealing with biographies and social studies content, certain specific vocabulary is necessary. For this reason, the readability of some of the stories in this book may be at a higher level than students can read independently.

How to Use the Stories

We suggest that you use the stories in this book for shared and guided reading experiences. Prior to reading, be sure to introduce any vocabulary that students may find difficult to decode or understand. A list of suggested words to teach is given on pages 3 and 4.

The Skills Pages

Each story is followed by four pages of activities covering specific reading skills:

- comprehension
- vocabulary
- making connections to students' own lives—comparison, evaluation, feelings
- making connections to the curriculum—mathematics, geography, written language, etc.

The content of the stories in *Read and Understand, Celebrating Diversity, Grades 2–3* requires that specific vocabulary be used. This vocabulary is often at a higher level than might be expected for the grade level. We suggest, therefore, that you introduce these words before presenting the story. It is also advisable to read the story to pinpoint additional words that your students may not know.

Diego's Tortillas 5
Diego, Abuela, tortilla, masa

Of the Earth 11
Native American

Signs of Friendship 17
sign language, interpreter, translating

A Letter to an Author 25
Faith Ringgold, asthma, tankas, college

Huynh's Chair 31
Huynh, Martinez, Mexico, South America, Africa, probably, furniture

Teresa's Family 38
Teresa, Mi estimada abuelita, Con mucho cariño, migrant, Pablo, tortillas, Tio Fernando

Athletes of Dance 45
Sports Illustrated, Coach, Aaron, martial arts, kata, weight lifter, muscular, Edward Villela, Carli, Analisa, ballet, leotard, floor barre routine, funky, Cavalier, duet, pas de deux, balanced

Moving Child 54
Sydney, Vicki, Kevin, scene, faraway

Seven Days of Kwanzaa 61
Kwanzaa, diary, author, illustrator, celebrate, celebration, Christmas, American, Africa, place mat, self-determination, responsible, creative

Michelle Kwan 69
Michelle Kwan, Brian Boitano, Nationals, secondhand, Olympic gold medal, challenge, determination, courage, failure, audience, dedicated

My Field Trip, Learning about the Navajo People 76
Navajo, Santa Fe, New Mexico, Palace of Governors, adobe, Native Americans, turquoise jewelry, Kayenta, kinaalda, ceremony, tostada, hogans, powwows, Monument Valley Navajo Tribal Park, monoliths, pattern

Borrowed from Iran 84
Bezhan, Iran, American citizen, accused, Dedar, Shayon, Mr. Tayebi, Farsi, aerospace engineer, education, pange, turban, chessboard, commented, checkmate, shah mat, shish kebab, gushfilli, sopaipilla

Diego's Tortillas

The bell rang. Diego dashed out the door of the school. "Maybe Abuela and I can make tortillas today," he thought. Diego raced off to his grandmother's house. He lived there with his mom, brother, and sister.

He opened the door to the warm smell of fresh tortillas. He had been begging Abuela to teach him how to make tortillas. She had agreed. She also warned him. "Making tortillas is not as easy as it looks."

"Hi, Abuela!" shouted Diego.

"Hello, Grandson," Abuela cheerfully answered.

"Can we make tortillas today?" asked Diego.

"Sure, we can. I think you want to take over my job!" said Abuela.

Soon the kitchen was filled with the sound of clanging bowls. Abuela used her hands to do the measuring. But she showed Diego how to use measuring spoons. He put in just the right amount of everything. Salt, flour, lard, baking powder, and water went into the bowl.

Abuela showed Diego how to knead the masa, or dough. Soon it was ready to roll out. Diego's grandmother took a small, round clump of masa. She flattened it with the tips of her fingers. She sprinkled flour on the table. Then she set the clump of masa on the flour. She used the rolling pin to flatten the clump. Back and forth clicked the rolling pin. Diego watched every move Abuela made. Soon Abuela had made a nice round tortilla. She put it in the pan on the stove.

Now it was time for Diego to try. He took a clump of masa. He gently flattened it. He sprinkled flour on the table. Then he laid the flattened clump on the flour. Back and forth clicked Diego's rolling pin. It was harder than it looked! He tried and tried to make his tortilla round. But he just couldn't get it as round as Abuela's.

"Look, Abuela, mine isn't round like yours," cried Diego. "How do you make them so round?"

"I have been making tortillas for a long time, Diego," said Abuela. "Wait until you are as old as I am. Making round tortillas will be easy."

Diego kept rolling and rolling the masa. Finally, Abuela said, "I think your tortilla is ready to cook." She picked it up. They both noticed that the tortilla was shaped like a heart.

"Look, Abuela, my tortilla is shaped like a heart!" shouted Diego.

"I think I like heart-shaped tortillas better," Abuela said with a smile. "Will you teach me how to make hearts, Diego?"

Diego laughed. "Yes, Abuela, but it's not as easy as it looks!"

Celebrating Diversity • EMC 796

Name_____

Questions about *Diego's Tortillas*

1. Why was Diego in such a hurry to get home?

_____

_____

2. Name two ingredients used to make tortillas.

_____   _____

3. What was the hardest step for Diego when making the tortillas?

_____

_____

4. What did Abuela say to Diego when he could not make the tortillas just like hers?

_____

_____

5. Do Abuela and Diego like spending time together? How do you know?

_____

_____

_____

_____

Diego's Tortillas
Special Words

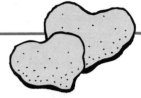

A. Draw a line to match each word from the story with its meaning.

rolling pin   • the Spanish word for "Grandmother"

masa   • to mix with the hands

Abuela   • flour, lard, water, salt, and baking
                                  powder mixed together to make
                                  tortillas

knead   • a tool used to flatten dough when
                                  making tortillas

tortillas   • round, flat food that is made out
                                  of dough

B. Use the special words above to complete these sentences.

1. Do you like corn or flour _____ best?

2. I can't make the pie until I find the _____.

3. We are learning some Spanish words at school. The other

   day I called my Grandma "_____." She didn't

   know what it meant.

4. Before we could shape the clay, we had to _____ it.

Diego's Tortillas
Tortilla Math

1. On Tuesday Abuela made a dozen tortillas. How many tortillas are in a dozen? _____ tortillas

2. Abuela's recipe calls for two cups of flour. Abuela wants to make two batches of masa. How many cups of flour will she use?

   _____ cups

3. One day Diego's brother and sister asked to make tortillas, too. Abuela said, "Okay." Diego made 3, his sister made 4, his brother made 2, and Abuela made 8. On the graph, color the number of tortillas each person made.

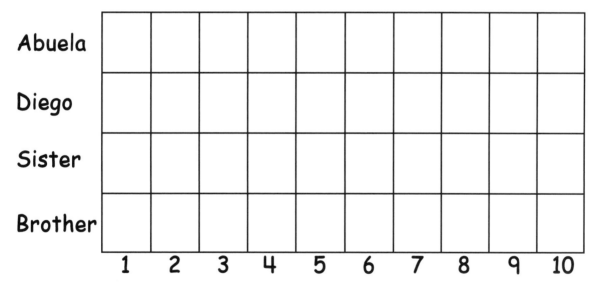

4. Look at the graph. How many tortillas did they make in all?
   _____ tortillas

5. Diego and his brother each ate two tortillas. His sister and Abuela each ate one tortilla.

   How many did they eat in all? _____ tortillas

   How many were left?_____ tortillas

Name_____

Diego's Tortillas
Write a Letter

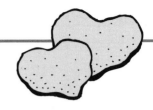

Write a letter to your grandmother asking her to teach you how to make her favorite cookies.

Misty jumped onto Mommy's lap. She loved the stories Mommy told her.

One day Mommy said, "Misty, today you tell me a story. You tell me about your day at school."

Misty thought for a while. Then she said, "Okay! Today our teacher was talking about names."

"What did she tell you about names?" asked Mommy.

"She said that sometimes people have a special story that goes with their names."

"Oh," Mommy replied. "Tell me more."

"Jack said he was named after his grandpa. Beth said she was named after her aunt. I wish I had a story about my name," said Misty.

"There is a story!" answered Mommy.

"There is? Tell me, please tell me," begged Misty.

"You know your long-ago grandpa was Native American."

"Yes, but what about my name?" Misty asked.

"I'm getting to that! He believed that names should be 'of the earth,'" continued Mommy.

"What does of the earth mean?" Misty asked.

"On the morning you were born it was very wet outside. The clouds were sitting on the land. You could almost see little drops of water in the air. The sun was just about to peek out over the earth. Suddenly you cried out. Your daddy and I looked at how beautiful you were. We looked at how beautiful the morning was. He remembered what your long-ago grandpa had said about names. Then Daddy thought of the perfect name for you.

"We named you Misty Dawn. Misty because the air was wet. Dawn because it was early morning. Both of your names are of the earth. Grandpa would have liked that.

"I looked at you and you seemed to smile at me. I knew then that Misty Dawn was the perfect name!" smiled Mommy.

"My name is of the earth!" cried Misty. "And I love it! Tomorrow I can share my name story at school, too!"

Celebrating Diversity • EMC 796

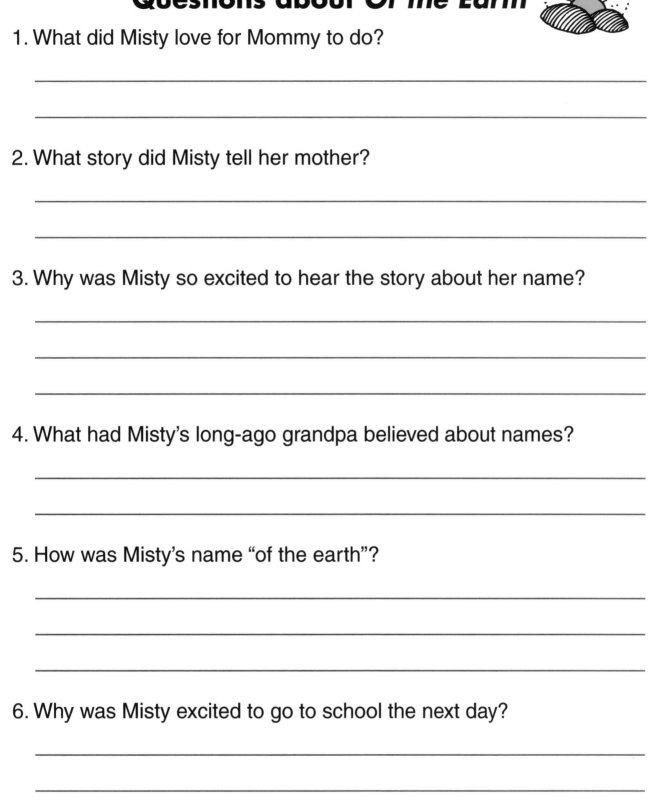

Questions about *Of the Earth*

1. What did Misty love for Mommy to do?

_____

_____

2. What story did Misty tell her mother?

_____

_____

3. Why was Misty so excited to hear the story about her name?

_____

_____

4. What had Misty's long-ago grandpa believed about names?

_____

_____

5. How was Misty's name "of the earth"?

_____

_____

_____

6. Why was Misty excited to go to school the next day?

_____

_____

Name_____

Of the Earth
Missing Words

This story has some words missing. Use words from the Word Box to complete the story.

Word Box						
special	earth	morning	dawn	mist	beautiful	perfect

My father and I took a _____ trip last July.

First we drove up into the mountains. We found a place to

camp beside a _____ lake. I'll never forget the

first _____. I woke up at _____.

It had been cold during the night. There was _____

lying on the ground. The _____ had a rich, wet smell.

I woke my dad.

"Come see what an awesome day it is!" I called.

Dad poked his head out of the tent. "You're right," said Dad.

"Everything is just _____."

Name_____

Of the Earth

My Name Story

Write a name story about your name. Your name story can be real or make-believe. Share your story with a friend.

_____

_____

_____

_____

_____

_____

_____

_____

_____

_____

_____

_____

_____

_____

_____

_____

_____

_____

_____

_____

_____

Name_____

Of the Earth
A Name Story Survey

1. Ask ten people outside your class the following question. Use tally marks to record each answer.

   Do you have a story about why your parents gave you your name?

   Yes   _____

   No   _____

2. Make a graph to record the tally.

3. Write a sentence that tells about the information on your graph.

   _____

   _____

 # Signs of Friendship

Britt rushed into the room with tears streaming down her face. Her face was red, too. Her hands flew through the air. She told her teacher and her sign language interpreter what had happened at recess.

"Nick grabbed my neck. He tried to push me down. I wasn't even playing with him."

The teacher put her arm around Britt. "Are you hurt badly?" she asked. When Britt faced a person, she could read their lips. Now, she read her teacher's lips and shook her head no.

"You are angry then. I don't blame you. I will talk to Nick." The teacher waited at the door for him to come in.

The two children, the interpreter, and the teacher went to a place in the classroom that was private. The teacher asked Britt to tell what had happened at recess. The interpreter said aloud what Britt said with her hands.

"Now, Nick," the teacher said. She was sure to turn so Britt could see her speak. "What is your side of the story?"

Nick couldn't help himself. He started to cry. "She was playing on the bars and so were my friends. She was screaming real loud. She came up and screamed in my ear." Nick put his hand up and touched his ear.

"Nick, all the children yell on the playground. I hear our class scream every day when the bell rings." The interpreter looked puzzled as she signed Nick's words to Britt.

"You don't hear how loud she screams. She hurt my ear!" Nick sobbed. "And I don't even know how to tell her to stop."

"Oh, Nick," the teacher said as she put her arm around him. "Britt cannot tell how loud her voice is. She did not mean to hurt you. She was probably just excited about the game she was playing.

"Britt has been deaf since she was a baby. She has never heard her own voice or anyone else's. Things that are loud and hurt our ears are sounds that she doesn't even realize are being made."

The interpreter was translating everything the teacher and Nick said. Britt's face looked very surprised.

"I didn't mean to hurt you, Nick," Britt signed.

"Nick, you have helped me see that we need to learn some things as a class. Thank you for being honest. You must not be rough with anyone on the playground. You need to use words to settle your problems."

The teacher went to the front of the room. "Boys and girls, I think we all need to learn some sign language so that we can treat each other with kindness and respect. Miss Land, will you help me teach the children some important signs?"

"I'd be glad to," Miss Land smiled as she finished signing for Britt what the teacher had said.

The children learned several signs that afternoon. They learned to say "yes" and "no." They learned to say "stop" and "hi." The children wanted to learn many more signs. The teacher said, "Only two more signs for today. Who knows some words we need to use with friends?"

Nick raised his hand. "We need to know how to say please and thank you—and sorry."

The teacher smiled at Nick. "I am so proud of you for thinking of that, Nick. I can tell that you want to be a good friend."

The next day was bitter cold. The children had an indoor recess. The teacher found Britt and Nick sitting at the computer together. They were playing a math game. The game was fast and exciting. The teacher heard Britt's voice getting louder. Then, it became quiet.

"Did you use your sign language, Nick?" the teacher asked.

"I said please," smiled Nick. He moved his open palm in a circle on his chest. "But I also said something in a language we both understand."

Nick put his finger to his lips. He was saying, "Sh!" Britt put her finger to her own lips and smiled. Then she signed "okay." The two friends went back to their exciting game.

Celebrating Diversity • EMC 796

Name_____

Questions about *Signs of Friendship*

1. Why did Nick hurt Britt?

_____

_____

2. How was Britt able to understand her teacher?

_____

_____

3. What did the interpreter do to help Britt?

_____

_____

_____

4. Why did Britt scream so loudly?

_____

_____

5. What are some signs you use instead of words to tell others what you think? (For example, clapping when someone performs well.)

_____

_____

_____

_____

Signs of Friendship
Synonyms and Antonyms

A. Make a circle around the pairs of words that are **antonyms** or opposites. Make an **X** on the pairs of words that are **synonyms** or mean the same thing.

push	pull	baby	adult
tell	explain	back	front
scream	whisper	loud	soft
up	down	quick	fast
shout	yell	touch	feel
hear	listen	before	after

B. Write two sentences using the words above.
Use a pair of **antonyms** in one sentence.
Use a pair of **synonyms** in the other sentence.
Then underline the words you used.

1. _____

_____

2. _____

_____

Name_____

Signs of Friendship
Friendly Words

If you had a deaf classmate like Britt, what words and phrases would you want to know how to sign?

Make a list. Tell how each word or phrase would make you a better friend.

1. Can you play? So I could let her know I wanted to do things
   with her.

_____

_____

_____

_____

_____

_____

_____

_____

_____

_____

_____

_____

_____

_____

_____

_____

Name_____

Signs of Friendship
Wordless Messages

There are many ways that we tell others what we think and feel without using words. For example, hugs tell people that we care about them.

Draw a picture that shows a way to say something without words. Then write a sentence under the picture that explains what the gesture, expression, or sign means.

_____

_____

A Letter to an Author

Dear Faith Ringgold,

    Hi. My name is Sara, and I am in the third grade. Our library teacher, Mrs. Brock, read your books to us. She told us about your life. We learned about how you started drawing and writing stories for children. Mrs. Brock said we could write to you.

    We learned that you had asthma when you were little. Many times you couldn't go to school. You had to stay in bed. I have asthma, too. But I can go to school most of the time. When I am sick, I like to draw and make things with cloth, just like you did.

    We learned that your mom was a dressmaker. She helped you learn to sew. My mom said that sewing bits of cloth together is called "piecing." Lots of people make quilts this way. She told me that quilt making was a job of slave girls long ago. Our teacher said your drawings are really story quilts that you painted. I learned that they are also called tankas. That means "paintings framed in cloth." I bet it is easy to carry your paintings. You can just roll them up!

I really like to draw, too. I want to be a teacher when I grow up. I learned that you teach at a college when you are not writing stories.

My teacher said that sometimes people are not treated fairly because they are a girl or are a different color. I think it was wrong that some people said you couldn't write stories or paint pictures. I'm really glad you didn't listen to them.

I loved your book <u>Tar Beach</u>. My favorite picture is the one on the cover. If I lived in an apartment, I would lie on a mattress on the roof and pretend to fly, just like the girl did. Please write more stories about when you were a little girl.

I liked what you said: "If I really, really want to, I think I can do anything." My mom tells me that all the time.

Your friend,

Sara

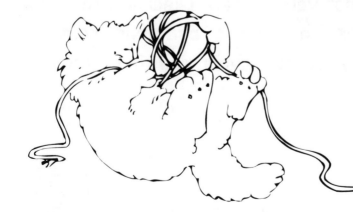

Celebrating Diversity • EMC 796

Questions about *A Letter to an Author*

1. Why is Sara writing a letter to Faith Ringgold?

   _____

   _____

2. Why was Faith Ringgold not able to go to school sometimes when she was little?

   _____

   _____

3. Why was Faith Ringgold able to roll her paintings to carry them?

   _____

   _____

4. Faith Ringgold has two jobs. What are they?

   _____

   _____

5. In the book Tar Beach, what does Sara's favorite picture show?

   _____

   _____

6. In your own words, tell what "If I really, really want to, I think I can do anything" means.

   _____

   _____

   _____

Dear Faith Ringgold,

A Letter to an Author
Vocabulary

A. Draw a line to match each word with its meaning.

piecing   ● a picture that tells a story

tankas   ● a person who sews clothes

pretend   ● sewing bits of cloth together

asthma   ● make-believe

teacher   ● a person who helps others learn

drawing   ● a disease that makes it hard to breathe

quilt making   ● paintings framed in cloth

dressmaker   ● a job of slave girls

B. Find the vocabulary words above in this word search.

```
w i p h s d r e s s m a k e r p l
y h r a p r q v a n a s p o l b x
c x e t e a c h e r r t i u j m e
n g t e y w m l o e b h z c o p w
o y e s d i a m k b c m w o p v m
g h n w x n t a n p t a n k a s s
u d d c i g r i p i e c i n g h j
t q u i l t m a k i n g m o n g e
```

Name_____

Dear Faith Ringgold,

A Letter to an Author
A Story Quilt

A story quilt, or **tanka**, is a set of drawings that tell a story. In the boxes below, draw a story about your favorite animal.

Note: Make this lesson real by actually mailing the letters. You can mail them to the publisher. Many authors have their own Web sites. Send the letters to them via e-mail.

Name_____

A Letter to an Author
A Letter to My Favorite Author

Write a letter to your favorite author asking questions about how he or she started writing stories for children.

_____

Dear _____ ,

_____

_____

_____

_____

_____

_____

_____

_____

_____

Sincerely ,

_____

Huynh (Who-yan´) rarely chose to read. That was until Mrs. Martinez's third-grade class. She read so many stories from the pile of books on her desk. Books took Huynh on many adventures. He had traveled to Mexico, South America, and Africa. As his teacher read, he would dream of faraway places. Before long he could hardly wait to read on his own.

One day there was an old green chair in one corner of the classroom. Mrs. Martinez said, "Class, I bought this chair at a garage sale. It will be a nice place to read during silent reading time. We will draw names to see who gets to sit in the chair."

Huynh waited each day for his name to get picked. At last his name was drawn. Quickly he took his book and walked to the chair. Before Huynh knew it, reading time was over! Day after day he crossed his fingers. "Please draw my name!" he wished.

One day his mother said, "Huynh, your father and I bought a new chair and sofa. You will no longer be able to snack in the living room."

"Okay, Mother," he answered. Then an idea struck him. Maybe he could take the old chair and sofa to school.

He asked, "Mother, what are you going to do with our old stuff?"

"I don't know. I will probably give it away," she answered.

"Do you think I could have it?" he asked.

"Why? Are you moving to your own apartment?" Mother teased.

"No, Mother. In Mrs. Martinez's class we have one big reading chair. If we had this chair and sofa, more of us would have a place to sit during silent reading," he explained.

"I don't know, Huynh. Do you think your teacher will want this old stuff?" she questioned.

"I could ask her. Please, Mother!" begged Huynh.

"Okay, but our new furniture is coming on Monday. Be sure to ask your teacher tomorrow," Mother said.

Huynh could hardly wait to see his teacher. He told her about the new furniture. He told her about the old sofa and chair. He asked Mrs. Martinez if they could move them into the reading corner.

"I'm not sure that a chair and a sofa will fit," Mrs. Martinez replied.

"But we would have more spots to sit at during silent reading," cried Huynh.

"Let's see how much room we have," said Mrs. Martinez.

Mrs. Martinez told the class about Huynh's plan for more silent reading places. Everyone was very excited. The students helped Mrs. Martinez measure the classroom space. The teacher asked questions about the size of the furniture. Huynh saw that both the chair and the sofa would make the classroom too crowded.

"Maybe I should just bring the chair," Huynh said.

Huynh's classmates all started talking at once. "Yes, maybe just the chair!" Huynh called his father. He agreed to deliver it that day.

After school Huynh helped Mrs. Martinez make room for the new reading chair. Soon his father arrived. The chair just fit next to the old green chair.

Mrs. Martinez said, "Huynh, thank you so much for giving us another reading chair!"

Huynh smiled from ear to ear. "Thank you for letting us have another chair. Now I will have twice as many chances to sit in the reading corner!"

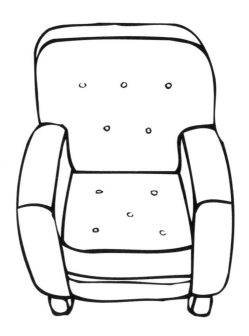

Name_____

Questions about Huynh's Chair

Cut out these sentences. Paste them in order on another sheet of paper to retell the story.

Huynh's father delivered the chair. It just fit next to the other chair.

Mrs. Martinez put a chair in the reading corner. Huynh hoped he would get to read in the chair.

Huynh was happy to have two chances to sit in the reading corner.

Mother and Father bought a new sofa and chair. They decided to give the old ones away.

Huynh listened to Mrs. Martinez read many stories about faraway places. He began to enjoy reading on his own.

Huynh asked his teacher if he could bring the old sofa and chair to school. After measuring, Huynh decided only the chair would fit.

Name_____

Huynh's Chair
Vocabulary

Here are groups of words from the story. In your words, tell what they mean.

1. rarely chose to read _____

_____

2. pile of books _____

_____

3. dream of faraway places _____

_____

4. garage sale _____

_____

5. crossed his fingers _____

_____

6. idea struck him _____

_____

7. silent reading _____

_____

8. smiled from ear to ear _____

_____

Name_____

Huynh's Chair
My Reading Place

Where do you like to go when you read? This might be at school or at home.

Write to tell about your favorite reading spot. Where is it? What is it like there? How do you feel when you are there?

_____

_____

_____

_____

_____

_____

_____

_____

_____

_____

_____

_____

_____

_____

_____

Name_____

Huynh's Chair
Design a Reading Corner

Your teacher has just given you an important job. You get to design a reading corner for the classroom.

First think about all the things you like to have in a reading corner. Then draw what this reading corner will look like.

Teresa's Family

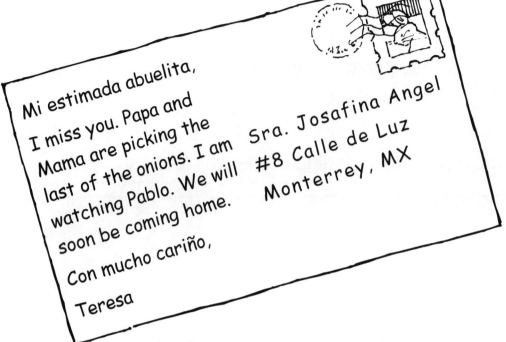

Mi estimada abuelita,
I miss you. Papa and
Mama are picking the
last of the onions. I am
watching Pablo. We will
soon be coming home.
Con mucho cariño,

Teresa

Sra. Josafina Angel
#8 Calle de Luz
Monterrey, MX

Teresa held her brother's hand. She dropped her postcard in the mailbox. She thought of how Abuelita's kitchen smelled of tortillas cooking. She missed her grandmother so much!

The walk back to the house was long and dusty. Teresa found a row of ants walking to and from their mound. They walked from place to place looking for food. It made Teresa think of her family. They would load into their cars and pickups. Then they would drive from place to place looking for work.

Her family worked as migrant workers. They traveled most of the year. They made a living working in the fields. Now they were picking onions. Teresa's aunt, uncle, and three cousins all traveled with them. Her cousins worked in the fields with the grown-ups. Someone needed to take care of Pablo. That was Teresa's job. She watched him catch a toad and hold it in his hands.

"Come, Pablo. It's time to take water to the field." Each afternoon Teresa took fresh water to her family. The day was hot. The sun was burning brightly. Teresa knew that her family would enjoy the water.

Pablo jumped from one row of dirt to another. Teresa followed behind. Her arms hurt from the heavy bucket. The cool water splashed onto her legs.

How tired her parents must feel after working all day. "I will help Mama make tortillas for dinner," thought Teresa.

Pablo ran ahead to show his cousins the toad. Teresa walked past a mound of gunnysacks filled with onions. The odor was strong and sweet.

Soon the bags would be placed onto a large truck. Then they would be taken to a weigh station. There the truck would be weighed. The bags of onions would be unloaded. Then the truck would be weighed again. Its weight would be subtracted from the first weight. That would tell what the onions weighed. The onions would be cleaned. Then they would be sold to grocery stores or food companies.

Mama gave Teresa a smile and scooped up Pablo. Papa and Tio Fernando finished filling a bag with onions. They were brothers. When they were boys, they had traveled with their parents, too.

On the way back to the house, Teresa picked up some onions. They had spilled from bags. Teresa knew they could be used in their dinner.

Every time Teresa's family went to a new job, they went to a new house, too. This house was old, but it was safe and clean. Mama would get angry when they had to stay in dirty or unsafe houses. One time Mama made them sleep in the car until she had cleaned the house.

Teresa put the onions on the counter. She went to help Pablo build a cage for his toad. When the cage was done, they found bugs for the toad to eat.

Papa and Tio Fernando sharpened the blades of their clippers. The clippers were used to cut the tops off the onions. Pablo showed his cousins the cage he had made. Teresa, Mama, and Aunt Sophia washed up to begin dinner. Mama turned on the radio. The music and the smell of tortillas made Teresa think again of her abuelita. Teresa heard Mama sigh, and looked up. They shared a smile. They were both thinking of home.

After dinner the grown-ups listened to the radio and talked. Teresa lay in her bed listening to the voices and music. She yawned. It would soon be time to go back south. Back to home and Abuelita.

Name_____

Questions about *Teresa's Family*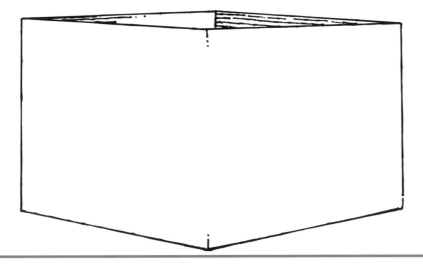

from Teresa

1. What did Teresa compare her family to? Why?

   _____

   _____

2. Why didn't Teresa work in the field?

   _____

3. Why did Mama have the family sleep in the car one time?

   _____

   _____

4. What things did the family enjoy at the end of a hard day's work?

   _____

   _____

   _____

5. If you were a migrant child, you would move from place to place.
   You might not be able to take many things with you. On the box
   below, make a list of the items you would want to take.

Name_____

from Teresa

Teresa's Family
Word Meaning

1. Teresa began her postcard with the words **Mi estimada abuelita**. This means "My esteemed grandmother." What do you think **esteemed** means? Circle any words you think are correct.

   honored   old   missed   respected   hardworking   admired

2. Teresa's postcard ended with the words **Con mucho cariño,** which means "With much love." Make a list of all the ways you might end a letter you would write.

   _____   _____

   _____   _____

   _____   _____

   _____   _____

3. **Abuelita** means "Grandmother" in Spanish. Make a list of all the names people use for their grandmother. You may include nicknames.

   _____   _____

   _____   _____

   _____   _____

4. Teresa's family works as migrant workers. What is a migrant? (Think about the word **migrate**, and remember that some birds migrate to warmer places in the winter.)

   _____

   _____

Name_____

Teresa's Family
Making Comparisons

Use pictures and words to compare yourself to Teresa.

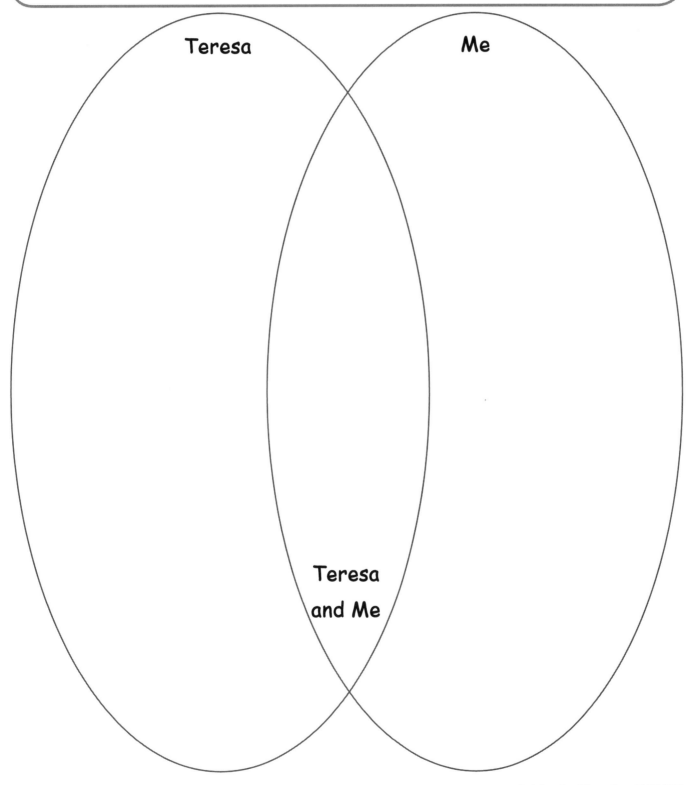

Teresa

Me

Teresa
and Me

Name_____

Teresa's Family
Problem Solving

Pablo likes to figure out how much things weigh. He made a balance scale, using a stick, string, and old milk cartons. It looked like this.

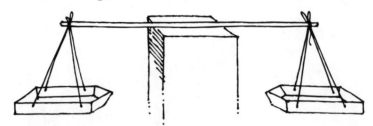

1. Pablo filled an old toy truck with beans. He wanted to find out how much it weighed. He discovered that the truck with beans weighed the same as 8 rocks.

   Draw a picture to show this.

2. Pablo dumped out the beans and weighed just the truck. It weighed the same as 5 rocks.

   Draw a picture to show this.

The beans weighed the same as 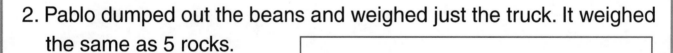.

Write a number sentence to show how you got your answer.

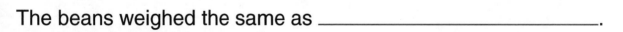

Athletes of Dance

Coach went around the circle. He asked each child, "Do you play a sport outside of school?"

"I play soccer," said Jimmy.

"I do, too," Frank chimed in.

Others named football and basketball. Some talked about bike riding and roller blading. A few hiked with their families. One girl was a swimmer.

It was Aaron's turn. "I am a dancer," he said.

The whole class began to giggle. "Dancing isn't a sport," Jimmy snorted. "You've got to be kidding!"

Aaron felt like crying. He got up and left the circle. Coach let him go.

Later, Coach went over and talked to Aaron. "I think you are right, Aaron. Dance is both a sport and an art. If the class knew some things about dance, they would understand. Is it okay with you if I teach them?" Aaron nodded.

"Get out there and play now," Coach grinned. He patted Aaron on the back.

The next day the children again sat in a circle in the gym. This time Coach showed them a magazine cover. "Does anyone know what magazine this is?" he asked.

"It's *Sports Illustrated*," said Frank. "My dad gets that magazine at home."

"I get *Sports Illustrated for Kids,*" said Carli. "I share it with my brother."

"Great," said Coach. "Look carefully at this person on the cover. Tell me what sport he plays." He held up the picture for all to see.

"He must be in martial arts," commented Zach. "He looks like he's doing a kata."

"He has big muscles, especially in his legs. I think he is in track and field. He could be a long jumper," guessed Hilary.

"I think he's a weight lifter," said Shawn.

"This muscular, strong man is named Edward Villela," said Coach. "He is a ballet dancer."

The room was full of surprised sounds.

Coach continued, "We have two special guest teachers today. They are young athletes who are already earning money in their sport. They are here to teach us the special things about their sport."

Coach opened his office door. "Jason and Analisa, please come meet our class."

First the girl came out. She was very pretty. Her hair was put up on her head. Her smile was wide and bright. She was dressed in a pink leotard and white tights. A sheer pink skirt was around her waist. She wore funny shoes that made her feet look very long.

Then Jason walked out. He had big muscles in his arms and legs. He looked really strong. He wore black tights and a white shirt. He wore black ballet shoes, too.

"We are dancers," Analisa began. "We have danced together as partners for ten years. We are now performing in a ballet called *The Nutcracker.*"

"I've seen that," Carli whispered.

"We've both been dancing since we were four years old. Dancing is our sport. It keeps us fit, strong, and healthy. We want to show you what it takes to be a ballet dancer."

For the next hour the class saw Jason and Analisa do many things. They showed the floor barre routine. It had many difficult moves. Both of them could do the splits and lie face down on the floor in that position. Jason could do the splits up the wall. They invited some of the children to try the barre. It was really hard!

Coach pulled out a large piece of wood. Jason slipped on his tap shoes and did a fast, funky dance. Analisa put on special dance shoes and did a slow, dramatic dance. Then they both pulled on jazz boots and did a fast-paced dance. It was like one you might see in a music video.

"How many of you could do that?" Coach asked.

"No way," said Jimmy. "I'd be out of breath."

"They have been saving the best for last," Coach announced. "Analisa is the Sugar Plum Fairy and Jason dances the role of her Cavalier. These are the two most difficult parts in *The Nutcracker*. They are going to dance their duet for you now. It's called a pas de deux."

The music began. Analisa turned and turned until the children felt dizzy watching her. "She's on her tiptoes. How does she do that?" Mary whispered.

Then Jason leaped onto the stage. He did high, jumping turns in a huge circle. He seemed to have wings on his feet. "He has better hang time than Michael Jordan," said Frank.

Then the two dancers came together. Jason picked his partner up again and again. Analisa spun over and over. She stood on her toes the whole time. At the end Jason picked up Analisa and threw her high into the air. She rolled her body several times before he caught her. Jason swung her down into his arms. She put her legs and arms in a position called a "fish." Just as the last note sounded, Jason raised his arms to the side. Analisa hung in the air, balanced on his leg. They kept their position because they were both so strong.

The class cheered wildly. Being so close to the dancers, they saw how hard their work was. They saw them breathing hard and sweating. They saw how strong and flexible they had to be.

"Now," said Jason. He quickly caught his breath. "Do you see why we say dance is both an art and a sport? Aaron, will you come up here?"

"Someday your classmate may be an athlete like these two," Coach said.

Aaron stood between the dancers and held their hands. They all took a bow.

Name_____

Questions about *Athletes of Dance*

1. Why did the class laugh at Aaron?

   _____

   _____

2. What did Coach do to make Aaron feel better after the class laughed at his answer?

   _____

   _____

3. Put these kinds of dances in the order Analisa and Jason danced them for the class.

   _____ ballet   _____ tap

   _____ dramatic   _____ jazz

4. How did Coach show that he respected Aaron's ideas?

   _____

   _____

5. How did Jason and Analisa show that they respected Aaron?

   _____

   _____

6. What made the students change their minds about dance being a sport?

   _____

   _____

   _____

Name_____

Athletes of Dance
Sports and More Sports

There are many sports listed in the story. Find all that you can and write them on the lines.

Then add to the list. How many different sports can you name?
Make a star beside the ones you have done.
Underline the sports you have seen on TV or in the movies.
Circle the sports you have read about.

_____

_____

_____

_____

_____

_____

_____

_____

_____

_____

_____

_____

_____

_____

_____

_____

Athletes of Dance
Write a Thank-You Letter

Pretend that Analisa and Jason came to your class to teach you about dance.

Write a thank-you note that explains what you learned.

_____

_____ ,

_____

_____

_____

_____

_____

_____

_____

_____

_____

_____

_____

Athletes of Dance
Graphing Sports

Make a bar graph of the sports your classmates play. Write in the names of other sports that are not shown. Be sure to ask all of the children in your class. Let each box stand for one person who plays that sport. You may need to count some people more than once if they play more than one sport.

Sports We Play

	baseball (T-ball)	dance	martial arts	soccer	swimming	no sport		
14								
13								
12								
11								
10								
9								
8								
7								
6								
5								
4								
3								
2								
1								

Moving Child

"Vicki, what are you doing?" Sydney, Vicki's best friend, found her sitting by the coats. "We're supposed to be outside."

Vicki was so startled that something fell from her hand. A sharp yellow pencil rolled across the floor to Sydney's foot.

"Sydney, please don't tell," Vicki said. She looked frightened. "I am writing my name on the wall behind the coats." She pulled aside a jacket. Sydney read "Vicki was here."

"Why would you do that?" Sydney wanted to know. Sydney liked to do the right thing.

Vicki started to cry. "I just found out that we have to move again. This is my last day of school."

"But you've only been here for two months. You've already gone to two schools before this one!"

"My dad has orders. We have to go. It is part of his job in the army."

"I will miss you so much," Sydney whispered. "We were just getting to know each other." She hugged Vicki.

That afternoon her mom and dad packed. Vicki helped watch her younger brothers and sisters. She was amazed at how fast they could be ready to leave. Already they were loading up a trailer. They would pull it behind their van.

Vicki looked around for her brother Kevin. She found him in the kitchen. He was sitting in a cupboard. "What are you doing, Kevin?" she asked.

Kevin looked surprised. A pencil skittered out of his hand and landed by Vicki's toe. "I'm writing all of our first names and the year in here. I'm putting it where no one will see. It shows we have been here in this house. You won't tell, will you?"

"I understand and I won't tell," Vicki told him.

By seven o'clock that evening the family was on its way. The children talked quietly. They shared what they would miss about the old house.

"I loved my bedroom because I could see the fog roll in from the sea," Vicki sighed.

"We liked having our own bathroom," the boys said.

"I liked catching lizards on the hill," said one of the girls.

"I liked my school and my friends." Vicki began to cry.

Their mom looked at their dad. Then she turned around to face the children.

"It is always hard to leave a place you have liked and move to a new one. We can't know yet what will be good or bad about our new home. We only know that we have each other. That will not change. If we take care of each other, we can find something good about living anywhere.

"Vicki and Kevin, I know that you worry about whether your friends will forget you. They won't. They will remember all the fun you had. Your teachers will also remember you because you were hardworking students. You were well-behaved and smart. You won't be forgotten.

"In our family, we will always remember what we did in the old house. We can remember any time we want. We can talk about it, too."

Mom reached back with something in her hand. She gave one to Vicki and one to Kevin. They were small pieces of paper with writing on them.

"When I learned that we would be moving again, I made sure to get the addresses of your friends. You have Sydney's address, Vicki. Kevin, you have Brian's. If you write to your friends, they will never forget you or the fun you had together."

The van rolled to a stop at a store.

"I think we need to buy some postcards and some stamps," Dad said.

The children piled out of the car. Kevin chose a football postcard for Brian. Vicki picked a desert scene for Sydney.

"Sydney has never seen the desert," Vicki told her mom.

"She will now," said her mom. "She'll see it through your eyes. That is one of the best parts of having a faraway friend."

Name_____

Questions about *Moving Child*

1. What did Vicki do that was wrong?

   _____

   _____

2. Why did Vicki have to move away?

   _____

   _____

3. Why didn't Vicki tell on her brother Kevin?

   _____

   _____

4. Why did Vicki and Kevin write their names in hidden places?

   _____

   _____

5. Why did their father stop the van?

   _____

   _____

6. Was Sydney right not to tell on Vicki for writing her name? Was Vicki right not to tell on her brother? Tell why you think so.

   _____

   _____

   _____

   _____

Name_____

Moving Child
Adding Endings

A. Add **-ing** to the words below to spell a new word. Then write the new words.

Remember…

        sometimes you double the final consonant,

        and sometimes you drop the final **e**.

If you are not sure of the spelling, look in the story. Each word appears there.

1. do   _____
2. sit   _____
3. write   _____
4. move   _____
5. load   _____
6. run   _____
7. catch   _____
8. live   _____
9. work   _____
10. have   _____

B. Write one sentence that uses **two** of the **-ing** words you wrote above.

_____

_____

_____

Name_____

Moving Child
Saying Good-bye

Have you ever moved away or had a good friend who moved away? Write how you felt when that happened.

If you have never had that experience, imagine that you have. Tell what you might feel and think.

_____

_____

_____

_____

_____

_____

_____

_____

_____

_____

_____

_____

_____

_____

Name_____

Moving Child
Make a Postcard

Here's what to do.

1. Cut out the "postcard" below.

2. Turn the postcard over. This is the front.

3. Pick a place your family has visited that is far from your home. Design the front of a postcard that you might send a friend. Make it colorful and interesting.

4. On the other side, write what you might tell your friend about that place. There is not much room to write. Think carefully about what to say.

5. Address the postcard to your friend.

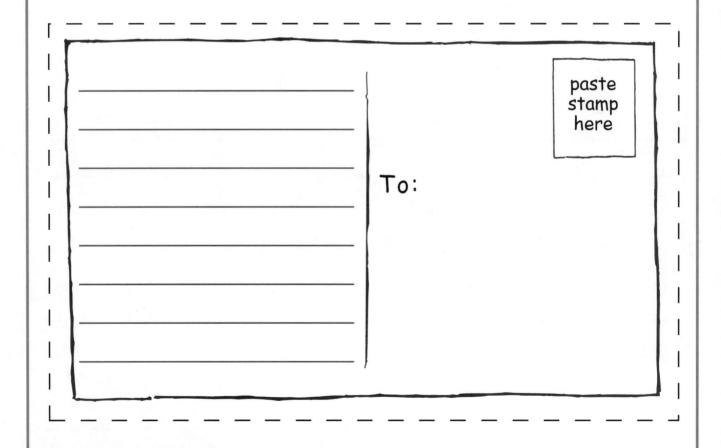

 # Seven Days of Kwanzaa

December 25

Dear Diary,

   It is Christmas Day. I am so excited to have a new diary. I can't wait to write every day about things that happen. I can write about things that are important to me, too. It will be fun. I think I will draw some pictures to go with the words. When I grow up I want to be an author and illustrator. My diary will be a good place for me to start.

December 26

Dear Diary,

   Today is the first day of Kwanzaa. Kwanzaa is a holiday that our family celebrates after Christmas. Father said this holiday is not very old. It started in America. The holiday is seven days long. Each day our family talks about ideas that came from Africa. Today Mother put out the special straw place mat with pretty patterns. We put one ear of dried corn on the place mat for each child in the family. We lit a black candle to celebrate our family being together. We laughed and talked and shared stories. It was fun.

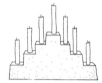

December 27

Dear Diary,

     Today is the second day of Kwanzaa. Father says today we will celebrate self-determination. I'm not sure what that means. I do know that this will be a day of learning. It is important to do things that we are good at. We can also work on things that we want to get better at. Today I am going to spend time learning to draw animals. We will also light the first red candle.

December 28

Dear Diary,

     What a fun day! The third day of Kwanzaa was for celebrating working together and being responsible. The whole family worked very hard to clean our family room. Sometimes I fight with my sister. But today we really had fun working together. We each tried our best. It felt good to finish our job. When we were done, we lit one of the green candles. I am really excited about tomorrow.

December 29

Dear Diary,

Yea! Today is the fourth day of Kwanzaa. We have been saving our coins for the whole year. Every person in the family has put coins into the glass jar for this day. Today we counted the money and decided what we will buy. The family gift must be something that everyone can use and enjoy. After lots of talking, we decided to buy a CD of African music. It is a good choice. We can listen to it alone or together. It was also fun to light another red candle. We were happy to see how fast our money grew.

December 30

Dear Diary,

I love to watch the Kwanzaa candles burning in the wooden holder. I like to remember what each color means. The black candle reminds us of Africa. The two red candles remind us to learn new things and to cooperate with others. The first green candle reminds us to work hard every day. I want to write stories. I know I will have to work very hard in school. I'm sure I can do it. Today we will light another green candle. We will talk about how working hard is part of being happy.

December 31

Dear Diary,

What a fun day this was! The sixth day of Kwanzaa is to celebrate being creative. When I feel creative, I love to write stories and poems. I also like to draw and color pictures. My sister likes to dance and make up songs. Some of her songs are really silly. She makes us laugh. My brother likes to build things with wood. Mother played the piano. We all sang. Father played his African drums. This was a red candle day. We have one candle left to light. It will be an exciting day.

January 1

Dear Diary,

This is it! The last day of our celebration! On the seventh day of Kwanzaa we celebrate faith. Mother says that faith is believing that good things will happen. I can hardly wait for our feast. Many of our aunts and uncles will join us for the day. We will give our family presents we have made. I have written a story about my grandmother. I drew special pictures to go with it. I will give it to Mother and Father. We will light the last green candle. Father will remind us what the other candles mean. We will eat, sing, dance, and laugh. I will write more tomorrow.

Questions about *Seven Days of Kwanzaa*

1. There are seven days to celebrate Kwanzaa. Here are some things the family in the story does during that time. Write the number of each day on the correct line.

   _____ The day of learning

   _____ The day of counting money to buy a family gift

   _____ The day to think about hard work that makes you happy

   _____ The day of working together

   _____ The day to put out the straw place mat and dried ears of corn

   _____ The day of eating, singing, dancing, laughing, and giving gifts

   _____ The day to do creative things

2. Tell what you would do on each of these days of Kwanzaa.

   Day Two

   _____

   _____

   _____

   Day Six

   _____

   _____

   _____

Name_____

Seven Days of Kwanzaa
Vocabulary

A. Write the number of each word on the line in front of its meaning. The first one has been done for you.

1. celebrate   __3__ looking forward to

2. diary   _____ a person who writes the words for a book

3. excited   _____ doing your job

4. responsible   _____ a person who draws pictures for a book

5. creative   _____ money like pennies, nickels, and dimes

6. illustrator   _____ to have fun on a special day

7. coins   _____ making something from your own idea

8. author   _____ a blank book in which you write about things that happen

B. Choose words from the list above to fill in the blanks.

1. When I do a book report, I have to tell the names of the

_____ and the _____.

2. The class was _____ to

_____ Valentine's Day.

3. At home I am _____ for feeding the cat.

Name_____

Seven Days of Kwanzaa
Dear Diary

A **diary** is a blank book in which you write about things that happen. You can also write about things you think are important.

Choose a holiday you celebrate with your family or friends. Write a diary page that tells what you did. Write at least five sentences.

Dear Diary,

_____

_____

_____

_____

_____

_____

_____

_____

_____

_____

_____

_____

_____

Name_____

Seven Days of Kwanzaa
Ordinal Numbers

1. Certain number words tell the order of things. Draw a line from each numeral to the word that goes with it.

1	• sixth
2	• fourth
3	• seventh
4	• third
5	• second
6	• first
7	• fifth

2. Keesha emptied her pockets. She lined up the things in a row on her desk. Draw each thing in the correct box.

1st [ ]

The second thing was a pencil.   **2nd** [ ]

A paper clip was the sixth thing.   **3rd** [ ]

A little spinning top was the fifth item.   **4th** [ ]

The third thing was a penny.   **5th** [ ]

An eraser was the fourth item.   **6th** [ ]

First she placed a crayon on the desk.

"Mama," I said. "What happened?" I couldn't believe my eyes! I watched Michelle Kwan step off the ice. I knew her scores would be low. The TV camera showed her face. I could see that she knew she had lost the 1997 Nationals for skating.

I love to skate. When I first saw Michelle Kwan skate, I wanted to be just like her. She wasn't much older than I. I pictured myself doing her spins and turns. I could almost feel the air and hear my skates on the ice as I watched her.

After one show I bought a program. She wrote her autograph on it. She smiled and talked with us about skating.

I knew how hard it was for Michelle to become a skater. Her family did not have a lot of money. Michelle would use rented or secondhand skates for practice. She spent hours practicing instead of watching TV or playing with friends. But you could see from her face each time she stepped on the ice just how much she loved being there.

Now, after all the practice and the wins, Michelle had fallen twice. I just couldn't believe it! I looked at my mom. She knew how upset I was.

When Michelle was seven she watched Brian Boitano win an Olympic gold medal. She decided she would win an Olympic gold medal someday, too. That was how I felt when I saw Michelle skate. I loved to skate, but I also wanted to win.

Michelle's scores showed on the screen. They were low. The audience seemed saddened by her loss. It was as if we had all expected her to win. I turned off the TV. I didn't want to see any more.

I sat next to my mom and put my head on her lap. She stroked my hair. "Do you believe being great at something means you never fail?" she asked.

I thought for a moment. Could it be that winners sometimes fail? I had a sudden new fear. "Mama, do you think she'll always lose now?"

I could hear my mom smile. "Think about when you began skating. Did you ever fall down?" I laughed as I pictured my most "famous" fall. "Did you quit, or get up and try again?" Mom asked.

I remembered how I refused to give up. I got up and tried again and again. I knew Michelle Kwan wouldn't give up. I knew she would come back to win.

A year went by. It was time for the 1998 Nationals. I watched for every bit of news about Michelle. She looked ready for the contest. Michelle began her warm-up. Then it was time to begin.

I watched Michelle skate to the music. It was wonderful! The failure of last year was gone! The crowd roared as Michelle left the ice. She was back on top!

Later that year I watched as Michelle skated in the Olympics. I held my breath at each jump and landing. As she skated to her final pose, I leaped up and cheered. When it was over, she had won the silver medal.

I sat on the couch and hugged my mom. I thought back to when Michelle had lost the 1997 Nationals. It took a lot of determination and courage to come back on top. I knew it was not easy. But Michelle had met the challenge.

I used her example to battle my own failures. Sometimes those failures were on the ice. Other times they were with friends or at school. I know that by overcoming them I will continue to win. Now, on to the next challenge.

Questions about *Michelle Kwan*

A. Draw a line from the beginning of each sentence to its correct ending.

In 1997 Michelle Kwan   • used rented or secondhand skates.

When Michelle first began skating she   • won the Nationals.

Michelle won the   • lost the Nationals.

In 1998 Michelle   • silver medal at the 1998 Olympics.

B. Answer these questions.

1. What does the person telling the story think of Michelle Kwan?

_____

_____

2. What things did Michelle Kwan give up so she could skate?

_____

_____

3. How would you answer the mother's question, "Do you believe being great at something means you never fail?"

_____

_____

_____

Name_____

Michelle Kwan
Winning Words

Dedicated and **determined** are two words that describe Michelle Kwan.

Winner

Work with a partner to brainstorm other words and phrases that describe the qualities of a winner. Write your words on the trophy.

Name_____

Michelle Kwan
The Courage to Go On

Michelle Kwan met her failure with courage and the determination to go on.

Tell about a time when you failed. How did you overcome the failure?

_____

_____

_____

_____

_____

_____

_____

_____

_____

_____

_____

_____

_____

Michelle Kwan
Skating Figures

Skaters make certain figures on the ice to practice going exactly where they want to go. One of these figures is a **figure eight**. It looks like this.

Solve the problems below.
Then circle each problem whose answer has an **8** in the **tens** place.
Connect all the circled numbers to make a skater's figure eight.

64 + 27	51 + 28	47 + 36	74 + 18	32 + 46
75 + 18	27 + 62	28 + 36	58 + 25	39 + 39
38 + 15	44 + 64	63 + 19	176 + 15	243 + 27
329 + 462	155 + 327	761 + 217	242 + 238	186 + 212
231 + 619	435 + 355	519 + 365	707 + 136	196 + 202

My Field Trip
Learning About the Navajo People

My name is Sara. My class went on a week-long field trip to learn about the Navajo people. Then we went to a school in Kayenta, Arizona. I wrote in my journal during the trip. My teacher thought I should share what I wrote with you.

Day One:

I could hardly sleep last night. All I could do was think about the field trip. I'm a little worried about being away from home for so long.

The bus ride was boring. I spent the night at a high school in Santa Fe, New Mexico. I was so tired I didn't even mind sleeping on the gym floor.

Day Two:

I went downtown. Santa Fe is built around a plaza. It looked like a park to me. At one end of the plaza is the Palace of the Governors. The palace is a small adobe building. It was built in 1610. In front of the palace were Native Americans. They were sitting in a long row on the sidewalk. They had colorful blankets spread out in front of them. On the blankets were many things for sale. There was silver and turquoise jewelry. There were sand paintings. I saw leather items and handwoven blankets, too. Many of the people selling their crafts were Navajo. My teacher said this is how they made their living.

I arrived in Kayenta after dark and quickly got ready for bed.

Day Three:

The morning sun was shining through an open gym door. My teacher thought the sun would wake me up. I just pulled my sleeping bag over my head. My teacher found me and dumped me out of my bag.

The principal gave a tour of the school. Almost all of the students were Navajo. They learn the same subjects as I do. They also learn to speak, read, and write the Navajo language.

The principal pointed to a large painting on one of the school walls. The mural was of a girl running toward a morning sun. The principal said this was a painting of the kinaalda ceremony. This ceremony means that a girl has become a woman. The girl runs each morning for four days. At the end of the ceremony everyone eats from a large corn cake. The corn cake is baked underground.

Lunch at the school was good. I ate a fried bread taco. It looked like a tostada but was made with a flat piece of fried bread.

After lunch I visited a third-grade class. This is what the students told me:

They live in houses or traditional hogans. A hogan is a home made with logs, bushes, and mud. It has six or eight sides and a round roof. The door faces east. That is the direction of the morning sun.

Many of the students own one or two sheep. This is to help learn responsibility. Many of their families also own cattle.

They enjoy powwows. At a powwow people dress in their finest costumes. They play music and dance. They didn't always have powwows. They learned how much fun they were from the Plains Indians.

They enjoy playing a string game. The game is like Cat's Cradle. It is played only in the winter. If the game is played in the summer, a legend says that Spider Woman will tie the players' eyes shut.

They enjoy playing basketball. They play it every recess. We were invited to play a game. Then their teacher played a Native American flute. I wrote in my journal as she played.

Day Four:

I went through Monument Valley Navajo Tribal Park. The park has 1,000-foot red monoliths. They are made of red sandstone. They look like giant stone fingers pointing to the sky. I drew a picture to show my mom and dad.

Tomorrow I go back home.

Day Five:

I got on the bus and quickly fell asleep. That was until a boy who ate six donuts for breakfast threw up. The bus didn't smell very good after that.

Home at last! I was happy to see my mom waiting for me. I'll be happy to sleep in my own bed tonight. I learned many things while on the trip. And my journal will help me remember everything.

Name_____

Questions about *My Field Trip*

1. Sara slept in schools each night. Where in the schools did she sleep? What did the teacher do to wake her up?

   _____

   _____

2. Name three items that were for sale at the Santa Fe plaza.

   _____

   _____

3. What did the principal of the Navajo school say about the mural on the wall?

   _____

   _____

4. What is a monolith?

   _____

5. Why was Sara happy that she had written in her journal?

   _____

   _____

6. What did you find interesting about the students at the Navajo school?

   _____

   _____

Name_____

My Field Trip
What Does It Mean?

Write each word from the Word Box on the line in front of its meaning.

Word Box			
legend	ceremony	mural	hogan
turquoise	powwow	responsibility	monolith

1. _____ a greenish-blue stone

2. _____ a picture painted on a wall

3. _____ a ritual; acting out a belief

4. _____ a traditional Navajo home

5. _____ a sense of duty; the act of being
trustworthy

6. _____ a gathering of Native Americans

7. _____ a story passed down from a long time ago

8. _____ a tall, thin rock structure

Name_____

My Field Trip
Making Comparisons

Compare your life with that of the Navajo students.

1. Many Navajo students own sheep to help them learn responsibility. What responsibilities have your parents given you?

   _____

   _____

   _____

2. The Navajo students enjoy going to powwows. What activities, celebrations, or festivals do you enjoy attending?

   _____

   _____

3. Basketball is the Navajo students' favorite sport. What is your favorite sport?

   _____

4. One of the Navajo students' favorite lunches is fried bread tacos. What is your favorite school lunch?

   _____

5. The Navajo students learn the Navajo language and the English language. What languages do you know? If you know only one language, what other language would you like to learn?

   _____

   _____

Name_____

My Field Trip
A Navajo Blanket

The Navajo are known for their beautiful blankets woven of wool.

Color this blanket to make a pattern.

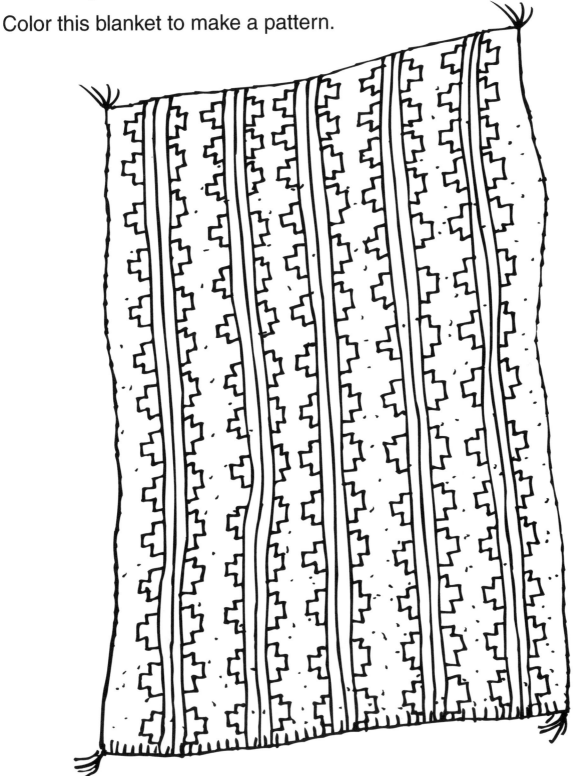

83

Borrowed from Iran

"You can't play!" shouted Tony. He pushed Bezhan hard.

Bezhan pushed himself up from the ground and dusted off his pants. He looked surprised. "Why can't we play?" he asked. He put his arm around his brother, Shayon.

"You guys are I-rain-ians," Tony snarled. "People like you hate Americans and try to hurt them."

"My dad is from Iran," said Bezhan. (He pronounced it Ee-ron.) "But my dad is also an American citizen. And so are we."

"I've heard you speak another language. Nobody understands it," Tony accused. "You are going to try to do bad things to us." Tony made both hands into fists.

"We don't want to do any bad things. We want you to know all of the good things about Iran. We have family in Iran that we love and who loves us. There are good things that come from Iran that you already know about. You just don't realize it."

"Yeah, I don't think so. There's nothing good about I-rain-ians." Tony walked off with his friends. The football game was over.

Celebrating Diversity • EMC 796

"We need to talk to Pedar (Ped-air)," said Shayon.

"You are right," Bezhan replied. "Pedar will know what to do." So they walked off to talk to their dad. He would help them figure out what to do next.

The next morning at school, the teacher told everyone about a special guest. "We are very lucky to have Bezhan, Shayon, and their father, Mr. Tayebi, here today. They will talk about Mr. Tayebi's homeland of Iran." She said the country's name the right way. That made Bezhan and Shayon smile.

Mr. Tayebi stood and introduced himself. "I am these boys' father. They call me **Pedar**. That means father in Farsi, the language of Iran. I am an aerospace engineer here in America. I have lived in this country for fourteen years. I have been a citizen for six years. I came to America to have a good education and to have more choices in my life. One of my sisters lives in the U.S. The rest of my family is still in Iran.

"There are many wonderful things about my homeland. I want to share some of them with you. There are many things about Iran that you share already."

Bezhan pulled out paper cups. Shayon helped him pour a fruity drink for all of the children.

"What do you call this?" Mr. Tayebi asked the children.

"Fruit punch," everyone responded.

"My goodness," he said. "Now you are speaking Farsi." The children looked confused.

"The American word punch comes from the Farsi word **pange**, which means five. Punch used to be a drink with five ingredients."

Mr. Tayebi held up a picture of a flower. "What is this?" he asked. Several children said, "A tulip."

"Right again," said Mr. Tayebi. "The word means turban in Farsi. Do you know what a turban is? It is a kind of hat. Doesn't the flower look like a little hat to you?"

Shayon had been setting up a chessboard on a desk. "How many of you know how to play chess?" he asked.

"We play chess on bad-weather days," the children said.

"Yeah," bragged Tony. "My dad is teaching me how to play at home. I'm good at it, too."

"I bet you are," said Mr. Tayebi with a wink. "Tony, what do you say when you win the game?"

"Checkmate!" grinned Tony. Everyone could see that Tony was proud that he knew this.

"You speak Farsi, too, Tony. That is wonderful. Our word for checkmate comes from the Farsi saying **shah mat**, which means the king is dead."

"Just wait 'til I tell my dad," Tony grinned. "I bet he doesn't know that."

Bezhan and Shayon began to pass out things to their classmates. Each child got a fruit kebab and a piece of what looked like sticky bread.

"This goes with your punch," said Shayon.

"You are eating food from Iran," said Mr. Tayebi. "We made fruit shish kebabs for you. The word **shish** means six in Farsi. See, there are six different kinds of fruit on your kebob. We also gave you cookies. These are called **gushfilli,** which means elephants' ears in Iran. We use lots of honey in these cookies, but no ears from elephants."

The class laughed. "This is sort of like a **sopaipilla**," said Juan. Mr. Tayebi nodded.

"Please enjoy your food, children. My sons and I want you to know that there are many good things from Iran. There are good words to use, good foods to eat, and good people to know. We hope that you will want to know more about people from Iran."

Tony got up out of his seat. He had eaten every bit of his food. "Come on, Bezhan," he said. He put his arm on Bezhan's shoulder. "Let's go play some chess. When I beat you, I'm going to say shah mat. The king is dead."

Bezhan smiled at his father and brother. Tony was going to be a good friend.

Name_____

Questions about *Borrowed from Iran*

1. Why do you think Tony didn't want Bezhan to play in the football game?

   _____

   _____

2. Where was Mr. Tayebi from?

   _____

3. Name the treats that the Tayebi family fixed for the class.

   _____

   _____

4. Why did Mr. Tayebi and the boys want to teach the class some words in Farsi?

   _____

   _____

5. Why did the class laugh when Mr. Tayebi told them the name of the honey cookies?

   _____

   _____

6. Why did Tony change his mind about playing with Bezhan?

   _____

   _____

Borrowed from Iran
Learning New Words

Find these Farsi words in the story. Tell what they mean and what word we use in English.

Farsi Word	What It Means	English Word
pange	_____	_____
shish	_____	_____
tulip	_____	_____
shah mat	_____	_____

Be a Word Detective

There is a food mentioned in the story that is <u>not</u> from Iran. It is from another country.

• Can you find the word? _____

• What country does the food come from? _____

• What kind of food is it?

_____

• Have you ever eaten this food? _____
  If not, how can you find out what it might taste like?

_____

Name_____

Borrowed from Iran

Now I Know

Pretend that you were in the class the Tayebi family spoke to.

Write a letter to your parents telling what you learned about people from Iran. Be sure to tell which things were brand new to you and which were familiar.

_____

Dear_____,

_____

_____

_____

_____

_____

_____

_____

_____

_____

_____

Love,

_____

 Celebrating Diversity • EMC 796

Name_____

Borrowed from Iran
Food from All Over

Many of our favorite foods came from other places in the world.

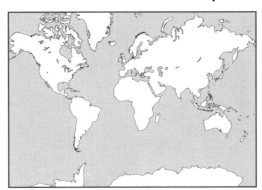

Find out which country these foods came from. You may need to use a dictionary or an encyclopedia.

Food	Country
taco	_____
sushi	_____
bratwurst	_____
lasagna	_____
burritos	_____
teriyaki	_____
fettuccine	_____
strudel	_____
baklava	_____

★Bonus: Can you find each country on a map of the world or
     a globe?

✦✦✦Light in a Dark, Silent World ✦✦✦

The little girl knew something was wrong with her doll. But she could not see what it was. She was blind. Her hands touched every inch of the doll. She found the torn dress. This made her so sad. She could not tell anyone how sad she felt. She could not talk or hear. Her sadness turned to anger. She threw herself down on the floor. She pounded with her fists and kicked with her feet. She screamed, but she could not hear her own voice.

Helen Keller was sick when she was just one-and-a-half years old. She had been blind and deaf since then. Her parents tried hard to give her a safe place to live. She had been a bright and lively baby. But they often did not know what to do to help her. Helen was now seven. She had not spoken a word since she was ill.

Helen felt her mother's arms around her. Helen felt so hot and angry that she did not stop her tantrum right away. Finally she calmed down.

Her mother led her to another part of the house. There she washed Helen's face, neck, and arms. She changed her dress and combed her hair neatly. Then she took Helen to the porch and had her sit in the shade.

Soon Helen could feel footsteps coming up the porch steps. She reached for her mother. Instead, someone else's hand took hers. She did not know this person. Her hands flew up the woman's arms to her face and hair. The woman sat very still.

The woman handed Helen something. It was a doll. Helen could tell by touch that it was beautiful. Then the woman did a very strange thing. She made squiggly movements with her fingers on Helen's hand.

So it was that Annie Sullivan came to live with the Keller family. She would become Helen's teacher. Miss Sullivan was using sign language to try to "talk" with her pupil.

It took many months before Helen understood what her teacher was doing. Once she understood what the signing meant, she learned quickly. She always wanted to learn more.

At ten Helen began to speak. She learned to read and write. She loved books. She loved to write her thoughts for others to read.

When she was twenty, Helen was able to attend college. This was a time when few women went to college. Helen's teacher was by her side, signing all the classes. Helen graduated with honors.

Helen devoted herself to helping people understand blindness. She raised money and wrote books. She gave many speeches about the needs of the blind and deaf. She met many of the most important people of her day.

All her life, she gave credit to Annie Sullivan. Her teacher had brought light and understanding to her once dark and silent world.

Name_____

Questions about *Light in a Dark, Silent World*

1. Why did Helen get so angry about her doll's torn dress?

   _____

   _____

2. How old was Helen when she became deaf and blind?

   _____

3. How could Helen "feel" someone coming up the porch steps?

   _____

   _____

4. What were the squiggly movements the teacher made on Helen's hand?

   _____

   _____

5. When Helen Keller grew up, what did she do?

   _____

   _____

   _____

6. How might Helen's life have been different if she had not had her teacher?

   _____

   _____

   _____

Light in a Dark, Silent World
Verbs

Words that tell what someone does or did are called **verbs**.

A. The verbs below are in the **present**. They tell what is happening now.

Change the verbs to the **past tense** so they tell what already happened.

Present	Past Tense	Present	Past Tense
reach	_____	love	_____
touch	_____	kick	_____
change	_____	wash	_____
live	_____	comb	_____

What patterns do you notice?

_____

_____

B. Now write the past tense of these verbs.

Present	Past Tense
know	_____
make	_____
hear	_____
take	_____

How are these different?

_____

_____

Light in a Dark, Silent World
Express Your Feelings

Helen did not know how to tell her family what she needed before she learned to sign and speak.

Pretend that you can share your thoughts with Helen without speaking. What advice would you give her for how to tell others what she is feeling?

_____

_____

_____

_____

_____

_____

_____

_____

_____

_____

_____

_____

_____

_____

Light in a Dark, Silent World
Sign Language Alphabet

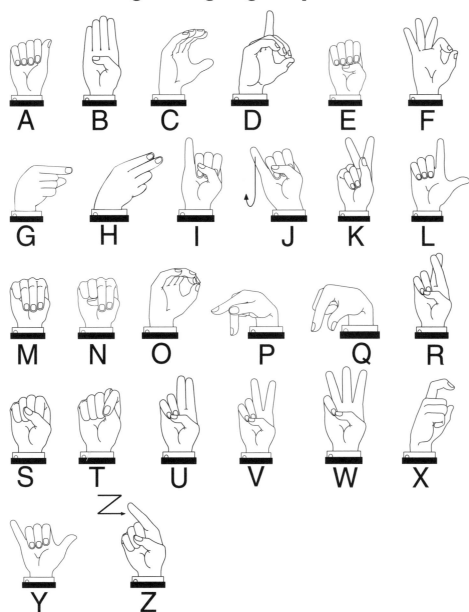

Find a partner. One person will read the words aloud. The other will try to spell them in sign language. Then switch places and practice again. Is it hard or easy for you to spell in sign language?

your name	doll	blind	teacher	deaf
porch	anger	hand	voice	college

 # Preparing for a Chinese New Year

It was one week before the Chinese New Year. My mom wanted me to help clean our house. She said a clean house would help us have a fresh start in the New Year. She also wanted a clean house just in case relatives visited.

I began sweeping the floor. As I swept dirt into a dustpan, I felt something. The handle of the broom bumped into my mom's best lamp. I turned just as the lamp leaned over the edge of the table. It looked as if it was getting ready to dive into a swimming pool. The crash on the floor even sounded like one of my dad's best belly flops.

I felt terrible about the broken lamp. I hoped I wouldn't have any more bad luck as I prepared for the New Year.

My mom said I should get my hair cut. This would help prepare me for the New Year. Mom turned on the electric clippers. She began cutting my hair. She only stopped to watch the exciting parts of a TV soccer game. My haircut was almost finished when a soccer player began kicking the ball toward the goal. With each kick the sportscaster yelled louder. My mom's hand on my shoulder became tighter and tighter. The soccer player took aim.

As the ball flew over the goalie's head, the clippers flew over my head. I could feel the clippers pressing against my scalp. A path was being cut from the back of my neck all the way to my forehead. Mom took a step back and looked at me. "Maybe I should cut your hair a little shorter this time," she said.

Going to school almost bald was no fun. Some kids teased me, but I was more worried about what my friends at Chinese school would say. Monday through Friday I go to regular school. On Saturday morning I go to Chinese school. This is where I learn to read and write the Chinese language.

On Saturday my teacher, Miss Oh, greeted me at the classroom door. I tried to walk past her, but she blocked my way. "New haircut?" she asked.

My best friend pointed at my head. "You're bald!" he shouted.

Other students started calling, "You're bald! You're bald!" My face turned red. Miss Oh gave them her "stop that!" look. She told everyone to sit down. She wanted us to draw **fai chun** poems. These are poems of good wishes for the New Year. I chose the poems "May you prosper" and "Good luck and lots of profit." I drew the poems on rectangular-shaped red papers.

We use a calligraphy brush to draw the characters for each poem. A character is a symbol that represents a word. It is more like a picture than letters.

I hoped these poems would bring me good luck. But no! I looked at my poems as I was putting away my brush. The brush only touched the lip of the inkwell, but that was enough. Ink began flowing like a river toward the edge of the table. "Oh, no!" I thought. I grabbed my two poems. I used them to stop the ink from dripping onto the carpet. My poems were ruined. But it was some good luck that the carpet wasn't ruined!

I was tired of having bad luck. On my walk home after class, I was sure bad luck was following me. As I walked up the steps to my house, the front door opened. A tall person picked me up and gave me a big hug. My uncle had come to celebrate the New Year with us. Perhaps I was going to have good luck after all.

Because my uncle was here, we had a wonderful fifteen-day New Year's celebration. We had a huge New Year's day meal. We placed oranges on our family altar to honor ancestors who had died. We went to a New Year's parade. There were floats and people dressed up like lions and dragons. We wore our new clothes and shoes. My uncle even gave me a red New Year's greeting envelope. It contained money. But the best thing of all was the red banner we hung on our front door. The Chinese characters said "Good Luck Has Arrived."

Questions about *Preparing for a Chinese New Year*

1. Name the three things the boy in the story did to prepare for the Chinese New Year.

   _____

   _____

   _____

2. Name three things the boy did during the fifteen-day Chinese New Year celebration.

   _____

   _____

   _____

3. Why did the boy's mom want to cut his hair short?

   _____

4. Why did the boy attend Chinese school?

   _____

   _____

5. What event in the story started to change the boy's bad luck to good luck?

   _____

   _____

Preparing for a Chinese New Year
What Animal Are You?

Did you know that you might be like a rabbit or a snake? That depends on your birth year. On the Chinese calendar, each year is named for an animal. People born in the same year are thought to be like that animal.

Write your birth year. Use the chart to find the name of the animal for that year and the words that tell about the animal.

My birth year is _____.

My animal is the _____.

My animal traits are being _____,

_____, and _____.

Animal	Years	Character Traits
Rat	1984, 1996	friendly, creative, and hardworking
Ox	1985, 1997	strong, loyal, honest
Tiger	1986, 1998	brave, earnest, hasty
Rabbit	1987, 1999	shy, quiet, humble
Dragon	1988, 2000	strong, imaginative, decisive
Snake	1989, 2001	tricky, subtle, controlled
Horse	1990, 2002	cheerful, talented, competitive
Sheep	1991, 2003	trusting, artistic, obedient
Monkey	1992, 2004	funny, inventive, mischievous
Rooster	1993, 2005	proud, confident, determined
Dog	1994, 2006	trustworthy, likable, loyal
Pig	1995, 2007	hardworking, caring, industrious

Are you like the animal that represents the year of your birth?
Write about it on another sheet of paper.

Name_____

Preparing for a Chinese New Year
My New Year's Celebration

1. What things do you and your family do to prepare for a New Year's celebration?

   _____

   _____

   _____

2. What things do you and your family do on New Year's Eve and New Year's Day?

   _____

   _____

   _____

3. What New Year's traditions do you and your family have that are similar to the Chinese New Year traditions?

   _____

   _____

   _____

4. The boy in the story was unlucky for most of the story. He became lucky at the end of the story. Tell about things in your life that you thought were lucky or unlucky.

   _____

   _____

   _____

   _____

Name_____

Preparing for a Chinese New Year
Following a Parade Route

You're the first person in the parade. Everyone will follow you as the parade winds through the city streets. To help you remember the route, draw the route on the map. Directions for the parade route are given below.

The parade starts on Kwan and 1st.

Move south to 1st and Ling.

Then go east to Ling and 2nd.

Next, go south to 2nd and Main.

Then go east to Main and 3rd.

Finally, go south to 3rd and Wang, where the parade ends.

The Vote

Mr. Bolinger collected the slips of paper. Jamie sat quietly in her wheelchair. Today her class would pick someone to go to student council meetings. She wanted to be that person. Ever since the accident, trying new things was hard for Jamie. Writing her speech was hard. Getting to the front of the class in her wheelchair was hard. But she was determined to run for the job.

All day it was hard to keep her mind on her schoolwork. She kept thinking about the slips of paper on Mr. B's desk. He had said that he would count the votes after school. Tomorrow he would tell the class who would go to the meetings. Tomorrow seemed like forever to Jamie.

At recess Jamie's friends told her she had done a great job on her speech. Jamie just smiled. At lunchtime she didn't eat much. She just wasn't hungry. The time seemed to tick by very slowly. At last the bell rang to go home. As she wheeled to the bus stop, her stomach growled. She remembered she hadn't eaten much lunch.

That evening Jamie's parents asked, "How was your speech?"

"It was hard to speak in front of the class," replied Jamie.

"Jamie, you know your speech was great," said Mom.

"And we know you did your best," Dad chimed in.

"Maria and Kendra thought I did a good job, too," said Jamie.

After talking to her parents, she felt better. Soon it was time for bed. Jamie knew that if she could fall asleep, it would soon be morning. When she woke up, it seemed like she had just gone to bed. The worries of the day before had made her very tired. In just a short time she would know who had won.

As the bus pulled to the bus stop, Jamie's stomach did a flip-flop. She wheeled slowly to the playground. She watched for her friends. Maria saw her and came running.

"I hope you won!" Maria shouted. Jamie couldn't answer. Her throat felt dry.

Just then the bell rang. The climb up the ramp seemed very hard today.

As she entered the classroom, she noticed the big sign. It said "Congratulations, Jamie!"

"You will go to the student council meetings for us!" said Mr. B.

Jamie started to shake as her classmates ran up to her. Her teacher gave her a pat on the back. She thought about how all her hard work had paid off. Being at school would be much easier today. Next time trying something new wouldn't be quite so hard.

Questions about *The Vote*

Read each statement. Mark **True** or **False.**

1. The students were voting for president of the class.

   ○ True   ○ False

2. It was hard for Jamie to write a speech and speak in front of her class.

   ○ True   ○ False

3. At home, Jamie felt better after talking to her parents.

   ○ True   ○ False

4. Jamie was not able to sleep all night.

   ○ True   ○ False

5. Maria did not want Jamie to win.

   ○ True   ○ False

6. Jamie lost the chance to go to the meetings for her class.

   ○ True   ○ False

7. Jamie's hard work had helped her win.

   ○ True   ○ False

Pick two statements above that are false. On the lines below, write them so they are true.

_____

_____

_____

Name_____

The Vote
Base Word and Endings

The words listed below are from the story. In the second column, write the base word. In the third column, write the ending.

Example:

	Base Word	**Ending**
seemed	seem	ed
1. speaking	_____	_____
2. collected	_____	_____
3. quietly	_____	_____
4. students	_____	_____
5. eaten	_____	_____

Compound Words

The words below are compound words from the story. Write the two words that make up each compound word.

Example: playground—**play**   **ground**

1. wheelchair	_____	_____
2. classmate	_____	_____
3. throughout	_____	_____
4. lunchtime	_____	_____
5. classroom	_____	_____

Name_____

The Vote

Some Things Are Hard to Do

The figure below is a **Venn diagram**. A Venn diagram helps to organize ideas.

In the left circle, write the things you have tried that were hard for you to do.

In the right circle, write the things that were hard for Jamie to do.

In the middle where the circles cross, write the things that were hard for both you and Jamie.

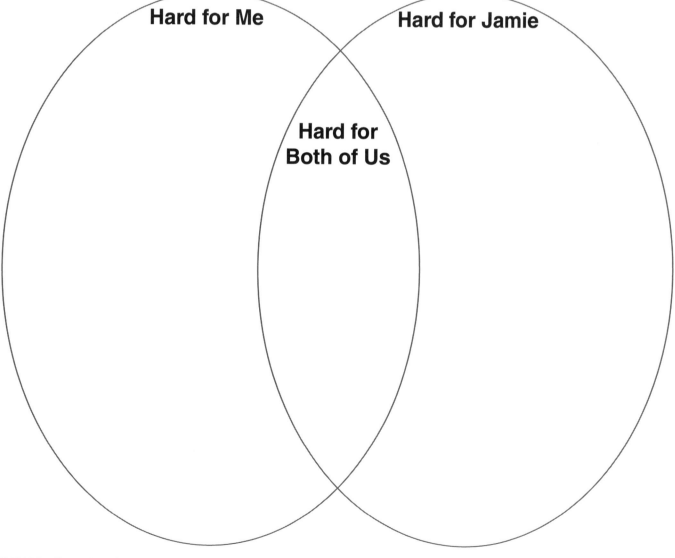

Hard for Me   **Hard for Jamie**

**Hard for
Both of Us**

                   Celebrating Diversity • EMC 796

Name_____

The Vote

How Many Votes?

Four students gave speeches, including Jamie. There are 20 students in Jamie's class. Each student cast a vote. Jamie was the winner.

Fill in the bar graph to show the information above. Use Jamie's name and three other names of your choice. On the graph, show how many votes each student received.

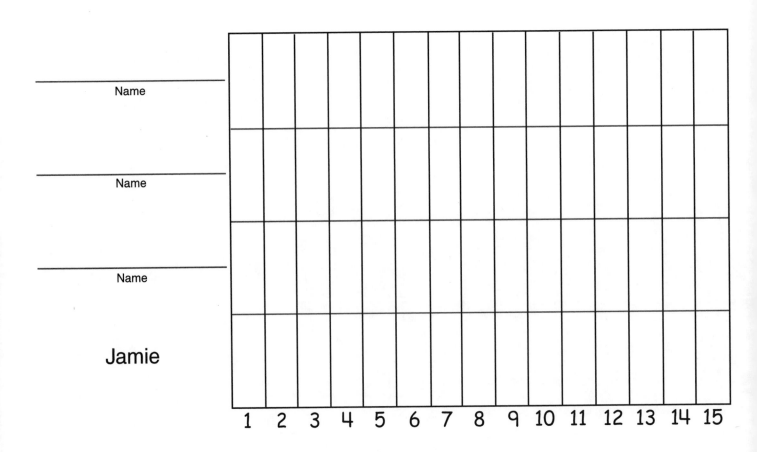

A Martin Luther King, Jr., Day Scavenger Hunt

My teacher loves to give homework. So I wasn't surprised when she gave us homework before Martin Luther King, Jr., Day. Don't get me wrong. I don't mind homework. I just hate the way she smiles when she gives it to us.

"Boys and girls, your homework is to go on a scavenger hunt." Miss Winter gave us her famous grin.

That sounded fun. I listened more closely.

"Your scavenger hunt takes place in a book. You will read a book of the life of Martin Luther King, Jr. You will find the scavenger hunt items in the book. Each item is something Dr. King would find important."

Miss Winter gave us the following list of items:

- a pair of wire-rimmed glasses
- a bus
- a podium
- an award
- a pair of shoes
- our class of students

The items were strange. That's the way scavenger hunts are. But why would our class of students be on the list? Martin Luther King, Jr., had died before any of us were born. He couldn't have known any of us.

I began reading the book right after my Saturday cartoons. I read that a man from India was important to Dr. King.

A long time ago India was ruled by England. The people of India didn't like that. Some people thought they should go to war. Mohandas Gandhi believed India could be free without fighting. He taught the people of India how to get what they wanted nonviolently.

Dr. King learned from Gandhi. He began to teach the people of the United States how to make changes peacefully.

I began to worry. I hadn't found any scavenger hunt items. I turned one more page. There was a picture of Gandhi. On his nose was a pair of wire-rimmed glasses! The glasses would be important to Dr. King because Gandhi wore them.

The next item on the list was a bus. I knew a bus would be important to Dr. King when I started reading about Rosa Parks. After a long, hard day at work, Rosa Parks was riding a bus home. The bus driver told her to give her seat to a white person. This was the city law. Rosa knew this was wrong. She said, "No!" The police came and put her in jail.

People were mad. Dr. King was also mad. He helped plan a boycott. Black people stopped riding the city buses. This went on for a year. The bus company lost a lot of money. The boycott worked. The laws were changed. Black people could sit anywhere they wanted on a bus. They didn't have to give up their seat to anyone.

I began reading about Dr. King's "I Have a Dream" speech. He gave this speech to 250,000 people in Washington, D.C. This was one of Dr. King's most important speeches. He told his dream of what life in the United States could be. Part of his dream was that his "four little children will one day live in a nation where they will not be judged by the

color of their skin but by the content of their character."

I saw a picture of Dr. King giving his speech. He was standing on the steps of the Lincoln Memorial. His speech papers were on a podium in front of him. Now I had my third scavenger hunt item.

Finding the award was easy. I read that Dr. King was given the Nobel Prize for Peace. He got the award because he taught people how to protest in a nonviolent way.

I read about a march in Alabama. Dr. King wanted to bring attention to problems that black Americans were having. During the march some white people became violent. But the marchers did not fight. This march helped people in the United States Congress decide to pass better laws.

Wait a minute, I thought. People needed shoes to march. Now I had all but one scavenger hunt item.

 I was finished with the book. I still didn't know why students in my class would be important to Dr. King. I thought for a long time. Then it came to me. Dr. King would be happy to know that my class is filled with many different kids. We have kids of many colors and religions. We play together. We work together. We are Dr. King's dream!

Questions about *A Martin Luther King, Jr., Day Scavenger Hunt*

1. Who influenced Martin Luther King, Jr., to use nonviolence?

   _____

2. Why was Rosa Parks important?

   _____

   _____

   _____

3. What was Dr. King's dream?

   _____

   _____

   _____

4. Why was Dr. King given the Nobel Prize?

   _____

   _____

   _____

5. Why would the class of students be important to Dr. King?

   _____

   _____

   _____

A Martin Luther King, Jr., Day Scavenger Hunt

Scavenger HUNT

Word Meanings

A. Write the number of each word on the line in front of its meaning.

1. podium   _____ a prize given for achievement

2. important   _____ acting with others to stop buying or using things

3. nonviolent   _____ a group of elected lawmakers

4. boycott   _____ the way a person feels, thinks, and acts

5. judged   _____ acting in a peaceful way

6. character   _____ meaning much; having value

7. award   _____ a stand where the speaker's notes are kept

8. Congress   _____ made up your mind; formed an opinion

B. Choose words from the list above to replace the underlined word or words in each sentence.

1. Students who do not miss any days of school are given a <u>prize</u>.

   _____

2. "Your friendship is <u>of great value</u> to me," she said.

   _____

3. "I want to be <u>thought of</u> by what I do, not what I look like,"

   declared the angry student. _____

Name_____

A Martin Luther King, Jr., Day Scavenger Hunt

What Would You Do?

Martin Luther King, Jr., believed in using nonviolence to solve problems.

Tell how you could be nonviolent in the following situations and still solve the problem.

1. You get up from your chair to sharpen a pencil. When you return, someone is sitting in your chair.

   _____

   _____

   _____

2. While standing in the lunch line, someone cuts in front of you.

   _____

   _____

   _____

3. While playing on the playground, someone calls you a bad name.

   _____

   _____

   _____

4. While playing a game, someone gets mad and hits you.

   _____

   _____

   _____

Name_____

A Martin Luther King, Jr., Day Scavenger Hunt
Draw and Tell

In the boxes below, draw each of the scavenger hunt items. Tell a friend how each item would have been important to Dr. King.

Louis Armstrong

My grandfather is so old fashioned! He doesn't like anything modern. He won't use a computer. He uses a typewriter. Does he drive a new car? No way! He drives a 1955 Ford. Does he listen to rock or hip-hop? Never! He listens to old jazz records. He says CDs aren't as groovy. He loves jazz. Even his alarm clock is set to a jazz radio station. He listens to jazz all day. Nothing but jazz.

One afternoon, my grandfather was listening to an old record. "Why are you listening to that old record?" I asked. "It sounds awful!"

He looked at me with his "Are you *my* grandson?" face. "Awful? This is one of the most important jazz musicians ever. If it weren't for Louis Armstrong, there wouldn't be much jazz today."

Then my grandfather said the words I hate. "You could learn a thing or two from. . .."

I sat down. My grandfather wasn't finished with me yet.

"You have it so good! Louis Armstrong was born poor. He had to work hard for everything he got. Growing up an African American in New Orleans in the early 1900s was no picnic. He hardly knew his father. His mother loved him. But she worked all day. At night she went to nightclubs called honky-tonks. His grandmother took care of him most of the time."

My grandfather took a big breath and went on. "Louis's childhood was not very happy. But he did enjoy listening to the music coming from the nearby honky-tonks. He could hear ragtime and blues from sundown to sunup. He even sang in the streets. People thought he was so good they gave him money."

Then my grandfather got this no-nonsense look on his face. "Don't get me wrong. Louis was no angel. He did a few bad things as a teenager. He stole money from people who were drunk. He also stole food and candy from small grocery stores.

"One New Year's Eve, he did something very dangerous. He wanted to celebrate by shooting a gun filled with blanks. Another boy began shooting blanks at him. Louis reached for his gun. A police officer stopped him. Louis was put in jail. The police officer asked the judge to put Louis in the Colored Waifs' Home. Life in the home was hard. But it was much better than being sent to a prison."

My grandfather smiled. "If Louis had not gone to the Waifs' Home, he might not have learned to play the cornet! Louis started playing the tambourine. Then he learned to play the bass drum and the alto horn. Finally, he learned to play the cornet. It wasn't long before Louis was the star of the band."

Then my grandfather patted his empty pants pockets. "When Louis was released from the home, he didn't have money to buy a cornet. The only work he could get didn't pay much. At long last a friend loaned him ten dollars to buy a cornet. Soon after, he was playing in bands around New Orleans. Louis played cornet for a long time. Later he changed to a trumpet. He said he liked its brighter sound."

My grandfather looked for a different record to play. I knew this meant he was about finished with me. But I was hooked. I wanted to know more about Mr. Armstrong. I asked, "Would you please tell me how Mr. Armstrong became famous?"

"You bet!" my grandfather said with surprise. "Louis became famous when he began playing in Chicago. He was with King Oliver's Creole Jazz Band. Then he played with Fletcher Henderson's band in New York. After that he began making records and movies. He toured the United States and Europe. Musicians around the world wanted to copy his style of jazz."

He leaned forward and said, "Louis had a long career. He never gave up. He worked hard to make his dream come true. Being poor didn't stop him from becoming one of the best jazz trumpeters ever!"

My grandfather began playing the record. We both sat back and listened to the sweet sounds of Louis's trumpet.

Maybe one day I will play the trumpet.

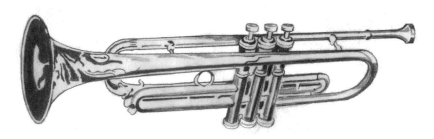

Name_____

Questions about *Louis Armstrong*

1. Where did Louis Armstrong grow up?

_____

2. What type of music did young Louis enjoy listening to when he was growing up?

_____

3. What good thing resulted from Louis being sent to the Colored Waifs' Home?

_____

_____

_____

4. How was Louis able to buy his first cornet?

_____

_____

_____

5. Tell about some of the things Louis Armstrong did in his long career.

_____

_____

_____

_____

_____

Name_____

Louis Armstrong
Musical Words

Fill in the sentences below using words from the Word Box.

Word Box			
jazz	musicians	trumpet	honky-tonks
tambourine	blues	cornet	ragtime

1. Louis Armstrong became famous for playing one type of instrument. At first he played a _____ , but later switched to a _____ because it had a brighter sound.

2. People who play an instrument or sing are called

_____ .

3. When Louis was growing up, he didn't have a television, radio, or record player. He did enjoy listening to the music coming from nightclubs called _____ .

4. The kinds of music young Louis listened to were the _____ and _____ .

5. Louis Armstrong played a type of music called _____ .

6. A _____ is an instrument that is beat and shaken.

Name_____

Louis Armstrong
Making Goals Come True

Louis Armstrong grew up poor and without much support from his family. Despite this, he had a goal of becoming a jazz trumpet player. With hard work and practice he accomplished this goal.

What life goals do you have? Do you want to become a musician, an athlete, a schoolteacher, a businessperson, or a dancer? Write your life's goal in the space below.

List below the things you need to do in school to accomplish your goal.

_____

_____

_____

_____

List below the things you need to do outside of school to accomplish your goal.

_____

_____

_____

_____

Name_____

Louis Armstrong
Writing the Blues

The **blues** is a type of music begun by black Americans in the early 1900s. Blues can be sung or played with instruments only. The blues tell a story. The story is usually about a person's problems. Here are the words to a blues song about homework.

> I've got the homework blues, homework every night.
>
> I've got the homework blues, homework every night.
>
> I'm working so hard, but I know it'll do me right.

Here's how to write your own blues song:

1. Think of some problem you have. Maybe your brother or sister is being mean to you. You hate doing the dishes. Or your hand aches when you pull weeds in the yard.

2. Write eight to ten words about your problem. Make sure you use the word **blues** in there somewhere.

3. Write the same line again. In the blues, the first and second lines are often the same.

4. Write a third line that solves the problem or makes fun of the problem. Remember to make the third line rhyme with the first two.

_____

_____

_____

_____

What does a great violinist look like? My grandparents took me to a concert. I imagined that I would see a tall white-haired artist standing on the stage. Was I surprised! The artist performing was Itzhak Perlman. Mr. Perlman is one of the greatest violinists to ever perform. His friendly face is framed with curly hair. He came onto the stage using crutches. His legs are paralyzed because he had polio when he was four. He sat in a chair in front of the orchestra. He put his violin under his chin. Then he began to play. It didn't matter what he looked like. His bow moved across the violin's strings. The melody sang out. Mr. Perlman became the music. I wanted to learn more about this incredible musician.

Itzhak Perlman was born in Tel Aviv. He was the son of Polish refugees. Itzhak began playing the violin when he was only three. He listened to the radio and imitated the music that he heard. His parents bought him a used violin. When he was four, Itzhak was stricken with polio. The disease left his legs paralyzed. Itzhak, unable to run and play, filled his days with violin practice.

He learned quickly:

When he was five, he enrolled at the Tel Aviv Academy of Music.

When he was ten, he gave his first recital.

At thirteen, he traveled to New York City to perform on American television.

The American audience loved his performance. Itzhak spent the next two months traveling across America, playing his violin. Itzhak wasn't satisfied. He wanted to improve his playing. He applied to the Julliard School of Music. His parents left Israel, and the family made New York their permanent home.

Today Mr. Perlman continues to amaze audiences with his beautiful music and his quick smile. He teaches and inspires young violinists. He lectures and records music. He also supports laws that help disabled people get into public buildings.

What is a great violinist like?

A happy father of five?

A disabled person in an electric wheelchair?

A busy chef preparing Chinese food in his kitchen?

A poker player laughing with friends?

A loyal Yankee fan cheering for a home run?

Itzhak Perlman is all of these and more. He is an artist with heart—he uses the violin to make music come alive.

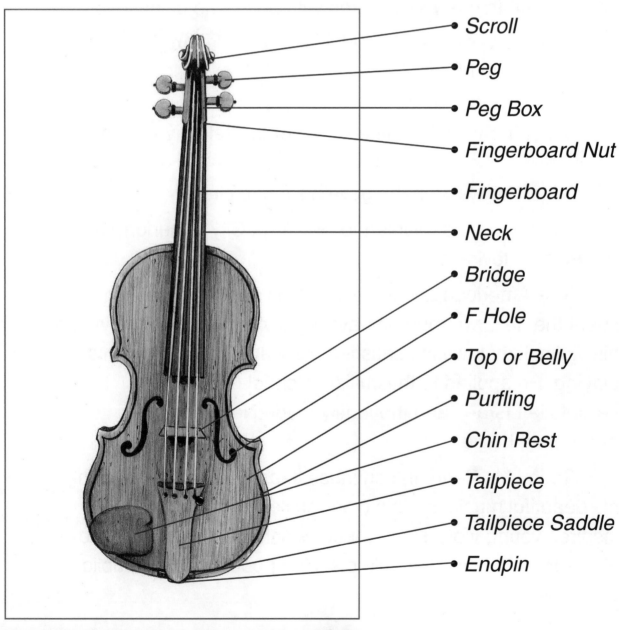

- *Scroll*
- *Peg*
- *Peg Box*
- *Fingerboard Nut*
- *Fingerboard*
- *Neck*
- *Bridge*
- *F Hole*
- *Top or Belly*
- *Purfling*
- *Chin Rest*
- *Tailpiece*
- *Tailpiece Saddle*
- *Endpin*

Name_____

Questions about *Itzhak Perlman*

Tell whether each statement is **true** or **false.** Then give details from the story to support your answer.

1. Itzhak Perlman immigrated to the United States.   _____

_____

2. Itzhak Perlman's life is an inspiration to handicapped
   people.   _____

_____

3. Musical artists must devote all of their energy to
   their art.   _____

_____

4. Children sometimes choose to study an instrument
   when they are very young.   _____

_____

5. A violin is a stringed instrument.   _____

_____

6. A violinist holds one end of the violin under his
   or her chin.   _____

_____

Name_____

Itzhak Perlman
Vocabulary

A. Draw a line to match the words with their definitions.

violin   • playing music in front of an audience

strings   • a musical instrument

bow   • a group of musicians playing together

concert   • a musical performance

orchestra   • stretched pieces of wire or catgut that vibrate to produce musical tones

performance   • a thin rod with strings used to play the violin

B. Use words from the list above to complete these sentences.

1. The girl learned to move the _____ across the _____ to produce beautiful sounds.

2. My brother will play in the band _____.

3. He carefully tuned the strings on the _____.

4. My mother plays a cello in the _____.

Name_____

Itzhak Perlman
Drawing a Diagram

Diagrams are simple illustrations of objects. Diagrams are often labeled to show the parts of the object.

Label this diagram to name the parts.

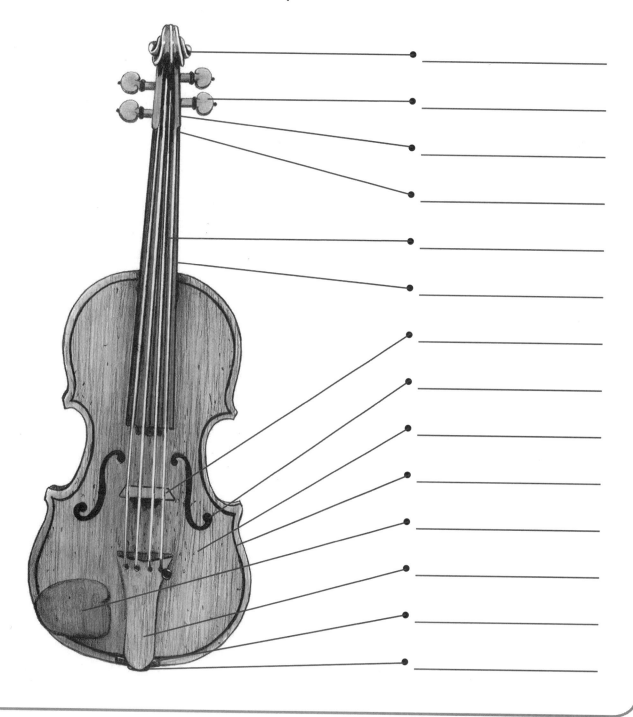

Name_____

Itzhak Perlman
The Music Around Me

Circle the words to answer the questions. Add your own answers.

Have you ever heard…

radio music?   music on a CD?   music at a concert?

music on TV?   music at a movie?   music on a tape recorder?

other? _____

Do you like to listen to music?   yes   no

Which music do you enjoy…

Classical?   Rock and Roll?   Rap?

Country Western?   Soul?   Spiritual?

other? _____

Do you play a musical instrument?   yes   no

If yes, what do you play? _____

Would you like to play…

trumpet?   _____   violin?   _____   piano?   _____

tuba?   _____   flute?   _____   drums?   _____

saxophone? _____   recorder? _____   guitar?   _____

other? _____

✯✯✯✯ Sacajawea, Girl Guide ✯✯✯✯

Sacajawea learned everything she knew at her mother's side. She watched carefully when her mother worked on a hide. She listened about how to search for roots to eat. She saw what plants her mother chose to make a sick person well. She learned how to find her way back from the woods. She learned how to use soft moss as a diaper in the cradleboard. She paid attention to animal tracks and signs. She could prepare and preserve food. Sacajawea learned the ways of her tribe, the Shoshoni.

Sacajawea was twelve when she was kidnapped by warriors from another tribe. She had been out gathering roots when she was taken. The people who took her were not cruel. But she was a slave. It was a sad and lonely life.

Then Sacajawea's life changed again. A French mountain man came into camp. He won a bet with the warriors. His prize was Sacajawea.

Now her path brought her to Fort Mandan. She stood back from the men who were talking. She was fifteen years old. Her first child would be born in a few months. Her husband was telling two white men that he and his family could help them.

The two men were explorers. Their names were Meriwether Lewis and William Clark. They were searching for a waterway to the Pacific Ocean. They were about to enter the mountains. Sacajawea could speak the languages of the mountain people.

Five months later, Sacajawea's little son was eight weeks old. She carried him in a cradleboard upon her back. They began the adventure that would take years. They would travel thousands of miles and map uncharted lands. They would discover new plants and animals that no white person had ever seen. Sacajawea would use her knowledge of survival in the wild to help them. She would help them build good relations with the mountain tribes. She would help them find food in the wild. She would nurse the sick and hurt. Through it all, she would be a loving mother to her son. She would protect him from every danger.

Lewis and Clark protected Sacajawea. They knew that she was vital to their trip's success. She stayed in the leaders' tent and rode in their best boat. They also gave her her own horse.

One day there was a rough wind on the river. The boat that Sacajawea's husband was steering filled with water. Many important supplies were washed into the river. Sacajawea's husband sat in the boat crying and praying to be saved. Sacajawea stayed calm. She caught many of the supplies as they floated away. Through it all, her son was on her back. Sacajawea earned even more respect that day.

Sacajawea fell ill on the journey. The explorers feared she might not live. But her strength and courage helped her again. She was able to travel on.

She helped to get fresh horses from her Shoshoni people. The explorers were able to meet peacefully with other tribes. They knew that a woman and her child would not travel with a war party.

When the group voted about where they would stay for the winter, Sacajawea was given an equal vote. This was long before women in the United States could vote.

Finally the long trip was over. Sacajawea's son was eighteen months old. Captain Clark offered to adopt him. Sacajawea agreed. Later, after Sacajawea died, Captain Clark raised her daughter as well.

Sacajawea was brave, strong, and smart. She knew the land. She knew the Indian tribes and their languages. She understood animals and plants. She got native foods for the explorers. She helped make the first exploration of the American Northwest possible.

The Westward route of Lewis and Clark from St. Louis, Missouri to the Pacific Ocean, 1804–1805

Name_____

Questions about *Sacajawea, Girl Guide*

1. Name three things Sacajawea learned from her mother.

_____

_____

_____

2. What happened to Sacajawea when she was twelve?

_____

_____

3. Tell three ways that Sacajawea helped Lewis and Clark.

_____

_____

_____

4. It was unusual that Sacajawea got to vote about where to camp for the winter. Why do you think Lewis and Clark let her vote?

_____

_____

_____

5. Why do you think Sacajawea agreed to let Captain Clark adopt her son and daughter?

_____

_____

_____

Name_____

Sacajawea, Girl Guide
Using Context Clues

The other words in a story or sentence will often help you understand the meaning of a new word. This is called **using context clues**.

A. Use the story context to help you match each word with its meaning.

cradleboard
- a trip

Shoshoni
- living in one particular place

waterway
- a place for which no map has been made

uncharted
- something to carry a baby in

journey
- to raise as one's own child

adopt
- rivers and lakes to travel on

native
- Sacajawea's tribe

B. Use the sentence context to figure out the meaning of each underlined word.

1. Some Indian tribes were <u>militant</u>. They would raid other tribes and capture their people and horses.

   ○ powerful   ○ living in the mountains   ○ ready to fight

2. Take care. The waters of this river are <u>treacherous</u> after the winter rains.

   ○ full of rocks   ○ unsafe   ○ running fast

Sacajawea, Girl Guide
A Trip Journal

Lewis and Clark kept a daily journal during their journey.

Pretend that you traveled with them and kept a journal, too. You can write as if you are one of the men. Or you can pretend to be Sacajawea or even her little son. Tell about what happened on one day of your journey. Tell how you felt about it.

Name_____

Sacajawea, Girl Guide
Mapping the Wilderness

As Lewis and Clark traveled west, they drew maps of the land they passed through.

Draw a map of the land you might have seen on one day of the trip. Put in rivers, mountains, and other important landmarks. Show your path on the map.

Use a map key to help explain your map to others.

Answer Key

Note: Open-ended activity pages are not listed in this answer key.

Page 7
1. He was eager to make tortillas with his grandmother.
2. Accept two of the following: salt, flour, lard, baking powder, water
3. rolling out the dough or masa
4. She told him it would be easy for him once he'd been doing it as long as she had.
5. Yes. Accept any well-considered response: They were happy to see each other; they laughed together; they liked to do things together.

Page 8
A.

rolling pin	the Spanish word for "Grandmother"
masa	to mix with the hands
Abuela	flour, lard, water, salt, and baking powder mixed together to make tortillas
knead	a tool used to flatten dough when making tortillas
tortillas	round, flat food that is made out of dough

B. 1. tortillas   3. Abuela
2. rolling pin   4. knead

Page 9
1. 12 tortillas
2. 4 cups
3.

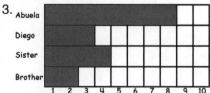

4. 17 tortillas
5. 6 tortillas
   11 tortillas

Page 13
1. Misty loved for Mommy to tell her stories.
2. Misty told about the name stories talked about in class.
3. Now she would have a name story to tell.
4. He believed that names should be "of the earth."

Page 14
special
beautiful
morning
dawn
mist
earth
perfect

Page 21
1. She had screamed in his ear.
2. She read the teacher's lips.
3. The interpreter used sign language to tell Britt what the teacher had said.
4. Because she was deaf, she could not hear how loud her voice was.
5. Answers will vary, but may include finger to the lips, smiles, pumping your fist, jumping up and down, pointing, or crooking your finger to "come here," etc.

Page 22
A.

push   pull
tell   explain
scream   whisper
up   down
shout   yell
hear   listen
baby   adult
back   front
loud   soft
quick   fast
touch   feel
before   after

B. Sentences will vary.

Page 27
1. Sara is writing a letter to Faith Ringgold because she is learning about her in school.
2. Faith Ringgold was not able to go to school sometimes when she was little because she had asthma.
3. Faith Ringgold was able to roll up her paintings because they were drawn on cloth.
4. Faith Ringgold's two jobs are illustrator and teacher, or author and teacher.
5. Sara's favorite picture shows a girl lying on a mattress on the roof.
6. Accept any reasonable answer.

Page 28
A.

piecing	a picture that tells a story
tankas	a person who sews clothes
pretend	sewing bits of cloth together
asthma	make-believe
teacher	a person who helps others learn
drawing	a disease that makes it hard to breathe
quilt making	paintings framed in cloth
dressmaker	a job of slave girls

B.

```
w i p h s d r e s s m a k e r p l
y h r a p r q v a n a s p o l b x
c x e t e a c h e r r t i u j m e
n g t e y w m l o e b h z c o p w
o y e s d i a m k b c m w o p v m
g h n w x n t a n p t a n k a s s
u d d c i g r i p i e c i n g h j
t q u i l t m a k i n g m o n g e
```

Page 34
1. Huynh listened to Mrs. Martinez read many stories about faraway places. He began to enjoy reading on his own.
2. Mrs. Martinez put a chair in the reading corner. Huynh hoped he would get to read in the chair.
3. Mother and Father bought a new sofa and chair. They decided to give the old ones away.
4. Huynh asked his teacher if he could bring the old sofa and chair to school. After measuring, Huynh decided only the chair would fit.
5. Huynh's father delivered the chair. It just fit next to the other chair.
6. Huynh was happy to have two chances to sit in the reading corner.

Page 35
Accept any reasonable answers. Possible answers include:

1. can read but chooses not to
2. books stacked on top of each other
3. think about places you have never been
4. selling things you no longer use
5. putting one finger on top of the other, hoping to be chosen
6. thought of something
7. reading in my head
8. a big happy face

Page 41
1. Teresa compared her family to a line of ants. They both followed each other from place to place looking for food or work.
2. Teresa needed to take care of her younger brother.
3. She thought the house was too dirty for her family to stay in.
4. They enjoyed listening to the radio and talking.
5. Lists will vary, but should include small items that are very portable.

Page 42
1. honored, respected, admired
2. Answers will vary, but may include: Sincerely, With love, Love, Your friend, Best wishes
3. Answers will vary, but may include: Grandmother, Grandma, Nana, Nonie, Grammy
4. *Migrate* means to move from place to place. *Migrant* workers go from place to place in search of work.

Page 44
Pictures should show:
1. Balancing the truck of beans with 8 rocks.
2. Balancing the empty truck with 5 rocks.

   The beans weighed the same as 3 rocks.

   The number sentence 8 − 5 = 3 should be written.

Page 50
1. The class did not think dance was a sport.
2. Coach told Aaron that he thought dance was a sport. He asked if it was okay with Aaron if he taught the class about dance.

3. __4__ ballet   __1__ tap
   __2__ dramatic   __3__ jazz
4. He invited two dancers to show the class how much athletic ability dance requires.
5. They asked him to take a bow with them.
6. The dancers showed that dance requires as much strength, flexibility, and stamina as any sport.

Page 51
Sports in the story are:

soccer	swimming
football	dancing
basketball	martial arts
roller blading	track and field
bike riding	weight lifting
hiking	

Page 57
1. She wrote her name on the wall in the closet.
2. Her father was in the army and had to move for a new job assignment.
3. She had done the same thing that he did; she felt the same way.
4. They wanted to leave some sign that they had lived and gone to school there. It was a way to feel remembered.
5. So the children could buy postcards and write to their friends.
6. Opinions will vary.

Page 58
A.
1. doing
2. sitting
3. writing
4. moving
5. loading
6. running
7. catching
8. living
9. working
10. having

B. Sentences will vary.

Page 65
1. 2
   4
   5
   3
   1
   7
   6
2. **Day Two:** celebrate self-determination; a day of learning; do things one is good at and work on things one wants to be better at

Day Six: celebrate being creative

Page 66
A. 3
   8
   4
   6
   7
   1
   5
   2

B. 1. author, illustrator
   2. excited, celebrate
   3. responsible

Page 68
1.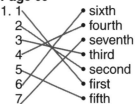
2. Pictures should be in this order:
   1st crayon
   2nd pencil
   3rd penny
   4th eraser
   5th top
   6th paper clip

Page 72
Correctly matched phrases will read as follows:

A. In 1997 Michelle Kwan lost the Nationals.

   When Michelle first began skating she used rented or secondhand skates.

   Michelle won the silver medal at the 1998 Olympics.

   In 1998 Michelle won the Nationals.

B. 1. She admires her greatly. Michelle is her role model.
   2. watching TV, playing with friends
   3. Answers will vary.

Page 73
Answers will vary, but may include words such as:
persistent, hardworking, not giving up, strong-minded, gutsy, firm, devoted, keen, enthusiastic, brave, courageous, strong-willed

Page 75

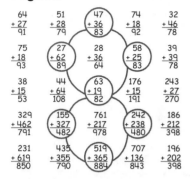

64 + 27 91	51 + 28 79	(47 + 36 83)	74 + 18 92	32 + 46 78
75 + 18 93	(27 + 62 89)	28 + 36 64	(58 + 25 83)	39 + 39 78
38 + 15 53	44 + 64 108	(63 + 19 82)	176 + 15 191	243 + 27 270
329 + 462 791	(155 + 327 482)	761 + 217 978	(242 + 238 480)	186 + 212 398
231 + 619 850	435 + 355 790	(519 + 365 884)	707 + 136 843	196 + 202 398

Page 80

1. in the gym; dumped Sara out of her sleeping bag

2. Any three of the following: silver and turquoise jewelry, sand paintings, leather items, handwoven blankets.

3. The principal said the mural showed a kinaalda ceremony.

4. a tall, thin rock structure

5. to help Sara remember her trip

6. Answers will vary.

Page 81

1. turquoise
2. mural
3. ceremony
4. hogan
5. responsibility
6. powwow
7. legend
8. monolith

Page 88

1. Tony had the idea that people from Iran wanted to hurt Americans.

2. Iran

3. pange, a fruit punch; fruit kebabs; gushfilli, a honey cookie

4. To show them that they already had some good things in their lives that came from Iran.

5. The name means "elephant ears."

6. Answers will vary, but may include the idea that now that he knew about Bezhan and Iran, he realized they had a lot in common and there was nothing to be afraid of.

Page 89

pange	five	punch
shish	six	shish kebab
tulip	turban	tulip
shah mat	the king is dead	checkmate

sopapilla

Mexico

It is a puffed pastry cooked in fat.

Answers will vary.

One might find a recipe and make sopapillas; one might order sopapillas in a Mexican restaurant.

Page 91

taco	Mexico
sushi	Japan
bratwurst	Germany
lasagna	Italy
burritos	Mexico
teriyaki	Japan
fettuccine	Italy
strudel	Germany, Austria
baklava	Greece, Middle East

Page 94

1. She could not tell anyone how she felt.

2. She was one-and-a-half years old.

3. She felt the vibration caused by the footsteps on the wood.

4. She was making signs to stand for words.

5. She wrote books and made speeches to help people understand blindness. She raised money to help blind and deaf people.

6. Answers will vary, but may include the idea that she would not have learned to communicate with people and might not have accomplished what she did.

Page 95

A.
reach	reached
touch	touched
change	changed
live	lived
love	loved
kick	kicked
wash	washed
comb	combed

Patterns—Some words just add *ed;* words that end in *e* just add *d* (or words that end in *e* drop the *e* before adding *ed*)

B.
know	knew
make	made
hear	heard
take	took

The words are spelled differently in the past tense.

Page 101

1. clean the house
   got a haircut
   drew fai chun poems

2. Any three of the following: ate a big meal, placed oranges on the family altar to honor ancestors, watched a parade, received an envelope containing money, put a Chinese character banner on the front door.

3. Because she needed to even out his bad haircut.

4. He learned to read and write the Chinese language there.

5. His luck began to change when he stopped the ink from dripping onto the carpet.

Page 104

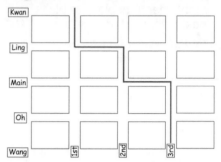

Page 107

1. False	5. False
2. True	6. False
3. True	7. True
4. True	

Accept true sentences about numbers 1, 5, or 6.

Page 108

1. speaking	speak	ing
2. collected	collect	ed
3. quietly	quiet	ly
4. students	student	s
5. eaten	eat	en

1. wheel	chair
2. class	mate
3. through	out
4. lunch	time
5. class	room

Page 115

1. Mohandas Gandhi

2. Rosa Parks refused to give her bus seat to a white person. This started the bus boycott.

3. Dr. King's dream was that people would not be judged by their color but by their character.

4. Dr. King was given the Nobel Prize because he taught people how to protest in a nonviolent way.

5. The class of students would be important to Dr. King because there were many different kinds of children, and they played and worked together.

Page 116
A. 7
   4
   8
   6
   3
   2
   1
   5

B. 1. award   3. judged
   2. important

Page 118
Drawing—a pair of wire-rimmed glasses

Gandhi wore wire-rimmed glasses, and Dr. King learned the importance of nonviolence from him.

Drawing—a bus

Rosa Parks didn't give up her seat on the bus, which brought about a bus boycott that Dr. King helped organize.

Drawing—a podium

Dr. King gave his "I Have a Dream" speech from behind a podium.

Drawing—an award

The award represents the Nobel Peace Prize given to Dr. King.

Drawing—a pair of shoes

The shoes represent the protest march from Selma to Montgomery, Alabama.

Drawing—a class of students

The class represents Dr. King's dream of all people being equal.

Page 122
1. New Orleans

2. jazz, ragtime, and/or the blues

3. This is where Louis Armstrong learned to play the trumpet.

4. A friend loaned him the money.

5. Answers will vary, but may include: played with King Oliver's Creole Jazz Band, played with the Fletcher Henderson band, made records and movies, and toured the United States and Europe.

Page 123
1. cornet, trumpet   4. blues, ragtime
2. musicians   5. jazz
3. honky-tonks   6. tambourine

Page 129
1. True—Itzhak and his parents moved from Tel Aviv to New York so he could attend Julliard.

2. True—Itzhak's legs are paralyzed but he doesn't let this limit his accomplishments.

3. False—While Mr. Perlman spends many hours practicing, he also enjoys cooking and going to Yankee games.

4. True—Itzhak knew that he wanted to play the violin when he was three.

5. True—The diagram of the violin shows that it has strings.

6. True—Itzhak put his violin under his chin and then he began to play.

Page 130
A. violin — a musical instrument
   strings — stretched pieces of wire or catgut that vibrate to produce musical tones
   bow — a thin rod with strings used to play the violin
   concert — a musical performance
   orchestra — a group of musicians playing together
   performance — playing music in front of an audience

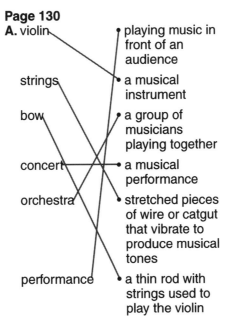

B. 1. bow, strings
   2. concert
   3. violin
   4. orchestra

Page 131
Diagram and labels should match those on page 128.

Page 136
1. Three of the following: how to prepare a hide, how to search for roots to eat, what plants can help sick people, how to find her way in the woods, how to use moss as a diaper, how to recognize animal tracks and signs, how to prepare and preserve food.

2. She was kidnapped by warriors from another tribe.

3. She helped them build good relations with Indian tribes, helped the sick and injured, and found food in the wilds.

4. She played an important role in the survival of the group. She knew the land, and her opinions were important.

5. Answers will vary, but may include the idea that she wanted them to have a better life and to get an education.

Page 137
A. cradleboard — something to carry a baby in
   Shoshoni — Sacajawea's tribe
   waterway — rivers and lakes to travel on
   uncharted — a place for which no map has been made
   journey — a trip
   adopt — to raise as one's own child
   native — living in one particular place

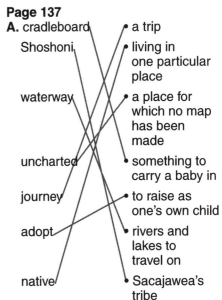

B. 1. ready to fight
   2. unsafe